D0889668

APPOINTMENT IN
JERUSALEM

MAX I. DIMONT

Appointment in Jerusalem

A Search for the Historical Jesus

St. Martin's Press   New York

Design by Maura Fadden Rosenthal

Library of Congress Cataloging-in-Publication Data

Dimont, Max I.
    Appointment in Jerusalem : the search for
the historical Jesus / Max I. Dimont.
        p.   cm.
    Include bibliographical references.
    ISBN 0-312-06291-5
    1. Jesus Christ—Historicity. 2. Bible.
N.T. Gospels—Criticism, interpretation,
etc. I. Title.
BT303.2.D53 1991
232.9′08—dc20   91-21449
                                        CIP

First edition
10 9 8 7 6 5 4 3 2 1

C O N T E N T S

Contents

INTRODUCTION

Though based on the scholarly works and sources listed in the bibliography, this book is not intended for scholars. It is intended as a popular book for people who have not read the Gospels but would like to know what they are all about, and for those who have read the Gospels yet are curious to know other views of Jesus. Both will discover that the Gospels are as multifaceted as a cut diamond.

The stance I have taken on religion is one that prevailed in the Roman Empire. In the paraphrased words of the historian Edward Gibbon, the Roman people believed all religions to be equally true, the Roman philosophers believed all religions to be equally false, and the Roman emperors believed all religions to be equally useful. Readers have the option to regard any or all views presented here as equally true, equally false, or equally useful—in proportion to their own preferences as to the weight of the evidence. This book is written not to subvert and not to convert, but to inform, to entertain, and to stimulate.

I concur with Ernest Renan who said: "For those who believe Jesus is the Messiah, he is the Messiah. For those who think he is the Son of Man, he is the Son of Man. For those who prefer the Logos, the Son of God, he is the Logos, the Son of God." I would add that for those who, like Rousseau, think of Jesus as a Hebrew sage, he is a Hebrew sage and for those who, as Voltaire, believe Jesus is a prophet, he is a prophet.

ACKNOWLEDGMENTS

It is my distinct pleasure to acknowledge a debt of gratitude to six individuals.

To critique my manuscript I did not want specialists in narrow fields but scholars with a collective background not only in theology but also in the humanities. I was fortunate to find six such eclectic individuals. They are: Christian B. Peper: B.A. Harvard, LL.B. Washington University, LL.M. Yale; past member, Visiting Committee, Harvard Divinity School. L. S. Oliver, D.D: President Emeritus, Nazarene Bible College; B.A. and M.A. University of Omaha, Colorado University, and Phillip University. Norman Katz: Ph.D. Massachusetts Institute of Technology, B.A. Yeshiva University, and Associate Studies in the Talmud. Judy Katz: B.A. Barnard College; Ph.D. in Classics, St. Louis University. F. Garland Russell: B.A. University of Chicago, B.A. and M.A. Cambridge University, LL.B. Yale Law School. Eric Bram: Associate Rabbi, Temple Israel, St. Louis; ordained, Hebrew Union College with an M.A. in Hebrew Letters; B.S. University of Illinois; Adjunct Professor of Philosophy, St. Louis University.

They critiqued my manuscript with severity, yet with a sympathetic understanding of the overall theme of this book. Collectively they brought to their task a comprehensive knowledge of history, theology, archaeology, mythology, law (ancient and modern), Greek, Latin, Hebrew, and, most of all, of the Gospels, Talmud, and the Classics.

It is said that "To err is human, to persist diabolic."

If errors still persist it is because I did not heed all their suggestions.

As in my previous works, no list of acknowledgments would be complete if it did not include my daughter Gail (Mrs. Michael Goldey) and my wife Ethel.

Gail—B. A. Radcliffe College, and a former editor at a New York publishing firm—as usual, edited her father's manuscript with a critical eye, relentlessly searching for missing transitions and antecedents, hunting for dangling participles and modifiers. Non sequiturs were heartlessly pierced with her sharp pencil. When a green flag pasted to the margin of a page appeared, I knew there was further research in store for me. To my chagrin, she was usually right. So, thank you, daughter, for the invaluable help you gave me. You are truly a "dutiful daughter."

As for my wife, this work would not have been completed if not the the unstinting help she gave me during the five years it took to research and write it. She was always at my side when I needed her, and at times even in my hair. She always had a steno pad ready to take dictation whenever a new idea occurred to me; she helped me re-edit every chapter, and retyped chapters as many as eight to ten times as they were revised. No computer or word processor could replace her. Often, however, I did feel like throwing the manuscript at her for she was not always the friendliest of critics. So to you, wife, go my special thanks for your love, patience, and dedication.

CHRONOLOGY

1 A.D. to 12	Jesus born in Nazareth, circumcised on the eighth day. Parents flee with Jesus for short stay in Egypt; return to Galilee. Four brothers and two or more sisters born. Jesus has his Bar Mitzvah in Jerusalem.
12 to 30	Jesus' whereabouts unknown for eighteen years.
30	Jesus is baptized; begins his public ministry; selects his twelve disciples. Rejected as the messiah by his parents and driven out of Nazareth by the townspeople. Jesus reveals himself as the messiah to his disciples. Transfiguration at Mount Hermon. Predicts three times that he will be arrested, tried, crucified, and risen in three days. Lazarus resurrected. Jesus heads for Jerusalem hailed as king by throngs of Jews. "Cleansing" of the Temple. The Last Supper. Judas "betrays" Jesus, disciples desert him, and Jesus is arrested. Hearing held by Sanhedrin. Jesus tried by Romans for treason; crucified on orders of Pontius Pilate. Interred in a tomb and found missing three days later.
31 to 33	Surviving disciples found Apostolic Church in Jerusalem. Early Christians, known as

Nazarenes, attend Jewish Temple, worshiping Moses and Jesus. Apostle Stephen stoned for blasphemy. Paul, a member of the stoning mob, becomes persecutor of Christians.

34 to 50   Paul has vision of Jesus on road to Damascus, becomes a Nazarene. Missions of Paul and Barnabas.

50 to 66   James, brother of Jesus, becomes leader of Apostolic Church. Strife between James and Paul. Paul "founds Christianity" with his Epistles, probably the first Christian writings. Executed by Romans in Rome.

66 to 70   Jewish War with Rome. Jerusalem gutted and Temple destroyed along with Apostolic Church. Nazarenes and Jews flee Judea.

70 to 75   Mark writes the first Gospel in Rome.

80 to 85   Matthew writes the second Gospel in Alexandria.

85 to 90   Luke writes the third Gospel in Antioch, Asia Minor.

90 to 110   Luke writes the Acts of the Apostles. Jews expel Christians from their synagogues, and

"Pauline Christians" expel the "Nazarene Christians" from their churches.

110 to 140   John completes the fourth Gospel in Ephesus, a Greek city in Asia Minor. Christianity now a distinct new religion, without Jews. Gnostic Christians begin writing their "heretic" gospels.

140   The first "New Testament" appears, edited by Marcion, a Gnostic, admitting only the Gospel of Luke and the Epistles by Paul as authentic Christian documents.

200 to 250   The "New Testament" expanded to include the Gospels of Mark, Matthew, and John.

325   Constantine converts to Christianity. Christian takeover of the Roman Empire begins.

367   The New Testament, as we know it today, canonized by Athanasius, Bishop of Alexandria.

400 to 500   Jerome (died 420) translates the Old and New Testaments from the Greek into Latin, a work known as the Vulgate, the basic Christian Bible until the Reformation. Gnostic Christians excommunicated and their gospels banned.

500 to 1000   Barbarians invade Europe. The Roman Empire falls. The Dark Ages descend upon Europe.

PART ONE

Myth, Faith, and Fact

Chapter 1

The Seven Faces of Jesus

Christianity, like Judaism, did not begin with a god or a king. Both religions were founded by humble figures born in insignificant corners of the world with an ancestry buried in obscurity. Judaism began about four thousand years ago, with a seventy-five-year-old pagan named Abraham, born in Babylonia, whose father was, according to legend, a merchant of idols. Christianity had its start two thousand years later, in 1 A.D., with a Jewish infant named Jesus, born in Nazareth, whose putative father was a carpenter.

Jesus lived thirty years—twenty-nine of them in obscurity. He entered history with a baptism at the beginning of 30 A.D.; a crucifixion ended his life before the year was spent.*

---

*Other, probably more specific dates, will be discussed later.

Though this crucifixion took place nearly two millennia ago, the drama is not yet over. Though his accusers are dead, witnesses vanished, and the judges dust, the trial of Jesus nevertheless continues. Though crucified, dead, and buried, he still lives in the faith of his followers. The death of Jesus, not his life, is so central to Christianity that without this crucifixion there would be no Christianity.

How should a historian view the phenomenon of this Jew Jesus to whom serfs, priests, and nobles have knelt in homage for nineteen centuries; in whose name people suspected of heresy were consigned alive to the flames of autos-da-fé; in whose image crusades were launched to convert by force people of other faiths to a creed abhorrent to them; yet in whose spirit was created Western Civilization, to me the greatest and most magnificent civilization in the history of mankind?

Who is this Jesus who, though there are over one billion Christians today, failed to make an impression on history until a century after his death; about whom there is not enough validated historical material to write a decent obituary; yet about whom more volumes have been written than about anyone else—over sixty thousand books just in the last hundred years.

From the Council of Nicaea in the fourth century to the Reformation in the sixteenth, everything written about Jesus was mostly a variation on the same theme—Jesus as the son of God. During those centuries, scholars prudently shied away from cross-examining the authors of the Gospel. One could be excommunicated or burned alive by a vigilant Church for examining too closely the validity of their assertions.

Thus, for the first 1700 years of the Christian era, ideology triumphed over evidence. Then, with the eighteenth century and the Age of Rationalism, evidence triumphed over ideology as scholars began to defy the Church* and contradict the theologians. Views other than that of Jesus as the son of God dawned on the scholarly horizon. From the eighteenth century to the present, this new breed of scholars speculated not only on the theological but also on the historical Jesus. The problem was, in the words of the Catholic historian Ernest Renan "how to preserve the religious spirit whilst getting rid of the superstitions and absurdities that form it."

In this three-century search for the historical Jesus, scholars uncovered six additional views—or faces—of him, all at odds with the official Church version and with one another.

But, the reader might object, if there hardly exist enough facts about Jesus to write a decent obituary, whence all the material from which scholars draw their information for these other divergent views of him? Interestingly enough, most of it is derived from the same source—the testimony given in the Four Gospels. How can this be so?

To draw its portrait of Jesus as the son of God, the Church selected those passages in the Gospels that supported its beliefs. Secular scholars, on the other hand, selected those passages not stressed by the Church, fashioning them into other concepts of Jesus consonant with their beliefs. But since all seven views originate from the same source, all represent, in a sense, the Gospel truth.

The seven portraits of Jesus etched by the Church and this new scholarship are varied and fascinating, giving rise to vexing questions. Is Jesus the Christian messiah, the literal son of God as averred by the devout? Or was

*Henceforth, whenever the word "Church" is capitalized it will refer to the Catholic Church only.

he a Jewish messiah, the son of man, stripped of his Jewish garments and robed posthumously in Christian vestments? Was he a Zealot who tried to wrest the throne of David from the Roman oppressors by force? Was he a "plotter" who masterminded his own crucifixion and resurrection in the sincere belief that he was the messiah? Was he an Essene, a member of an obscure Jewish religious sect that practiced a primitive form of Christianity a century before his birth? Or is Christianity the creation of another Jew, Paul, who shaped the historical Jesus in his vision of a theological Christ? Or was he a "Gnostic Christian," a libertine practicing occult pagan rites as claimed in the recently discovered Gnostic gospels? Finally, was Jesus perhaps a combination of all of them, some of them, or none of them? But no matter who avers what, no one disputes Jesus was a Jew.

The Four Gospels, however, are not only a great literary work but also a great mystery story. In the center of that mystery, which contains all seven interpretations of Jesus within one leitmotif, are the four enigmatic predictions he made to his disciples.

All four evangelists concur that, after stating that he must go to Jerusalem, there to fulfill his destiny, Jesus three times made the following four predictions: that he would be arrested by the Jewish priests; that he would be tried by the Romans; that he would be crucified by the Romans; and that he would be resurrected ("rise again," as he expressed it) in three days.

Several puzzling questions arise. At the time Jesus made these predictions he had done nothing to warrant either an arrest by the priests, or a trial by the Romans. Was he planning to provoke them to take such actions?

Another puzzle. The Romans crucified only seditious slaves and rebels against Rome. But, as Jesus was neither a slave nor at this point a rebel, did he plan to foment a revolt to merit such a predicted fate?

And the final puzzle. Why did Jesus predict a resurrection after three days? Why not after two days? Or four? Or one?

The Four Gospels affirm that all his predictions were fulfilled. This confronts us with a host of new questions. How were they fulfilled? Were they accidental or did God arrange for their fulfillment? Or did the evangelists write their own scenario and then retroactively attribute these predictions and fulfillments to Jesus?

Or did Jesus himself engineer events in such a way as to bring about the fulfillment of his own predictions? If so, how did he achieve it? And for what purpose? Like skilled mystery writers, the evangelists subtly reveal the clues to the fulfillment of each prediction as the story progresses.

This book not only will explore all seven faces of Jesus and his four predictions, but will also tell the incredible story of Jesus and his impact on Jews, Romans, and the future Western Civilization in the century from his baptism to the publication of the Gospel of John, and how, in that one century, five faithmakers—Paul, Mark, Matthew, Luke, and John—transformed an inglorious crucifixion into a glorious resurrection and laid the foundation for the future Christian conquest of the Roman Empire.

Chapter 2

Appointment in Jerusalem

The Gospels were not an easy scenario to write.

The evangelists—Mark, Matthew, Luke, and John— were four authors with a climax but no beginning and no middle. They had to structure a past for Jesus to explain the meaning of his death walk to Golgotha; thus the Gospels grew backward, in the shadow of the cross. The end had happened before anyone had thought of a beginning. This forced the evangelists to construct the life of Jesus, not out of consideration for facts, but to meet ends. The past had to explain the present.

The Four Gospels are the only documents in the New Testament that tell the story of the life and death of Jesus. They are a tour de force of literature and theology.

In Hitler's Germany with its racial laws, the four Gospel authors—or evangelists—would have been classified as three Jews and a pagan, three of them qualified can-didates for concentration camps. Mark, Matthew, and Luke were Jews who had converted to Christianity. John, though a Christian by birth, was a descendant of converted pagans.

Though the Gospel of Matthew is placed first in the New Testament, Mark's was the first chronologically, written in Rome between 70 and 75 A.D., about forty-five years after the death of Jesus. It is a skeleton biography, and probably the most historically accurate. One of its objectives was to whitewash the Roman participation in the crucifixion in order to shift the blame for it from the Romans to the Jews.

Matthew, the second of the four evangelists, was known as the "Christian Rabbi." He was a teacher who lived in Alexandria where he wrote his Gospel around 80–85 A.D., much of his material based on Mark. Matthew increased the number of miracles and added a virgin birth for Jesus and a genealogy linking Jesus to King David.

Luke, a physician, was a native of Antioch who wrote his Gospel in Greece sometime during the years 85–90 A.D. He died at the age of eighty-four, unmarried and childless. Like Matthew, Luke also borrowed heavily from Mark. It could almost be said that his Gospel is an enlarged edition of Mark's.

The fourth evangelist, John, is an enigma. Scholars believe that he wrote his Gospel in Greek, in Ephesus, around 110 to 120 A.D., if not as late as 140.

John had one purpose in writing his Gospel, and he stated it succinctly—to make sure that anyone reading it would believe that Jesus was the son of God. To achieve this, he abandoned history for theology. The reason for this is abundantly clear. John's Gospel was beamed not to the Jews, whom he had written off as unlikely can-didates for his brand of theology, but to the pagans, the future mass market for Christianity.

Scholars are forced to question the Gospel accounts of the life, ministry, and death of Jesus as history because, though the theology is impeccable, many of the facts are questionable—all four Gospels abound in improbabilities, impossibilities, and contradictions.

What Mark says is often contradicted by Matthew and Luke, who often contradict each other. John's Gospel differs even where the three other evangelists agree, which is not often. Because Mark, Matthew, and Luke, nevertheless, in the main, espouse one common viewpoint, their works are known collectively as the "synoptic Gospels," from the Greek, meaning a "seeing together." At times one is forced to take the word either of John or of the synoptic evangelists, for no compromise exists between their conflicting assertions.

After the death of Jesus, but before any of the Gospels had been written, tradition had given birth to two contradictory themes to explain the meaning of the life and death of Jesus. One was that of a divine predestination drama with God in control of events. The other was that of a deicide tragedy with Jesus the victim of evil forces.

In the first scenario there are no heroes or villains. Everybody—Mary, Joseph, the Holy Ghost, Judas, Pilate, the high priest, even Jesus himself—all do the bidding of God. Judas is as much the instrument of God's will as Mary.

This predestination theme, however, presented the evangelists with a dilemma. If the Jews did God's bidding, they were in essence God's chosen instrument for giving life to the religion the Jews were later to reject. This dilemma gave rise to the second scenario, in which the Jews were portrayed not as midwives to Christianity but

11

as participants in the death of Jesus. The evangelists skill-fully combined these two opposite themes of "predesti-nation" and "deicide" into a powerful three-act salvation drama.

The first act introduces the predestination theme. In it, all the dissident elements are gathered into a crescendo of action—from the birth and baptism of Jesus (which are seen as predestined events) to the rejection in Nazareth of Jesus as the messiah by his family and hometown.

The second act is a transition stage. It dramatizes the transformation of Jesus from doubt as to his future course of action to his bold decision to "go it alone"—that is, to travel his predestined path to death. Or, to paraphrase Jesus—I must go to Jerusalem there to fulfill my destiny.

The third act introduces the deicide tragedy. It is the finale wherein Jesus achieves his messianic crown through the twofold action of a crucifixion and a resurrection.

As background for the future entry of the biblical diagnosticians who will dissect the Gospels and introduce their six concepts of a historical Jesus, let us unveil the first portrait of Jesus as conceived by the evangelists—the messiah as the son of God.

But before we raise the first-act curtain on this pre-destination drama, we note that whereas Mark and John wade right in with the baptism of Jesus, Matthew and Luke offer a short prelude to that baptism. The stage setting for this prelude is a most modest one—a small town in Galilee named Nazareth, a heap of small huts built of cubes of stone and mud, hidden by time and geography in a narrow valley, 1200 feet above sea level. It is here in Nazareth that a Jewish teenage girl named Mary (her Hebrew name is Miriam), is engaged to a Jewish carpenter named Joseph, a descendant of the house of King David, a royal family branch fallen upon hard times.

Mary's tranquil pastoral life is shattered one day when the angel Gabriel comes to her and says, "Hail, O favored one, the Lord is with you." Though but a teenager, Mary is suspicious of such a greeting, troubled by the implication that it might be a euphemism for "pregnant." She boldly questions Gabriel as to "What sort of greeting might that be?"

Gabriel confirms her worst suspicions. "Do not be afraid, Mary," he says, "for you have found favor with God. You will conceive in your womb and bear a son."

Mary indignantly informs Gabriel that she is a virgin and that she has never slept with any man, not even her betrothed, her fiancé Joseph.

Gabriel springs the surprise of her life on her. He informs her that the impregnating agent was not her fiancé but the Holy Ghost. Though Mary is pregnant, Gabriel assures her she is still a virgin.★

But Mary's troubles were just beginning. She had her betrothed Joseph to contend with. Mary's coming home to tell Joseph that she was pregnant was an admission of adultery for which he could legally break his marriage contract.

When Mary's condition became known to Joseph, a pious Jew, he first thought of breaking off his engagement

★Matthew's and Luke's belief in Mary's virginity rests upon a misreading of Isaiah. Believing Isaiah had prophesied that the messiah would be born of a virgin, these two evangelists claim such a birth for Jesus. Alas, Matthew and Luke were not great Hebrew scholars. The word Isaiah uses is *almah*, which does not mean "virgin" but only a "young woman," who may or may not be a virgin. The Hebrew word for virgin is *betulah*, which Isaiah does not use.

13

and sending her back to her family quietly so as not to disgrace her. An angel came to her rescue explaining to him the role of the Holy Ghost. Joseph graciously accepted this explanation and married his pregnant fiancée. A grateful Church later sainted him for his consideration—one of six Jews in a panoply of Catholic saints who had never been converted to Christianity.*

The Old Testament prophets placed Matthew and Luke on the horns of a dilemma by providing two birthplaces for the messiah. On the hand, the messiah had to be born in Bethlehem to fulfill the prophecy in Micah (5:2) that the future messiah would hail from the hometown of King David. On the other, Jesus had to be from Nazareth to fulfill another prophecy in Hosea that the messiah had to be known as the Nazarene.

Both Matthew and Luke proved they had good Jewish "Talmud heads" on their shoulders. Matthew had Jesus born in Bethlehem to fulfill one prophecy, then had his parents move to Nazareth to fulfill the other.

Luke had another solution. His fulfilled both prophecies by having Jesus conceived in Nazareth but born in Bethlehem. This he did deftly, stating that in her last week of pregnancy, Joseph took Mary from Nazareth to Bethlehem for a Roman census-taking—a census for which there is no historical evidence.

Upon arriving in Bethlehem, Joseph and Mary were forced to spend the night in a shed reserved for animals, and here the virgin birth took place in a manger. On the eighth day Jesus was circumcised according to Jewish law, and until his death he ate only kosher** food.

---

*The other five were: the grandparents of Jesus; the parents of John the Baptist; and St. Simeon, the old man who held the baby Jesus in his arms.
**Food permitted by Mosaic Law.

When did the birth in the manger take place? According to tradition, Jesus was born in the year 1 A.D. Scholars dispute this date and claim Jesus was born sometime between 6 B.C. and 6 A.D., the date, depending upon which Gospel one uses as a guide.

Matthew and Luke did not consult each other when they compiled their chronologies linking Jesus to King David for they employed contradictory chronologies. Matthew should be the favorite of the feminists, for, whereas Luke has an all-male family tree for Jesus, Matthew admits four women. Many theologians, however, are indignant because he included among those four women a harlot (Rahab), an adulteress (Bathsheba), and an incestuous woman (Tamar)—not exactly an exemplary lineage for a messiah. The fourth woman, Ruth, got her second husband by solicitation, and some scholars suspect by premarital fornication. However, Ruth was the great-grandmother of King David; Bathsheba became the wife of King David and the mother of King Solomon.

Luke is the only evangelist to state that at the age of twelve Jesus appeared in Jerusalem, where he confounded the scribes with his astounding knowledge of the Torah, the Hebrew name for the Old Testament. This account makes it sound as if Jesus had some kind of Bar Mitzvah, a ceremony heralding the entry of a Jewish male into the full obligations of Jewish law.

After this bar mitzvah, Jesus disappears from the pages of all four Gospels for eighteen years until his return at the age of thirty. What follows is an explosive mixture of history, theology, and faith—a time bomb activated by his coming baptism and set to explode a year later at Golgotha with the fallout of a new religion, a new civilization, and a new world order.

The messianic history of Jesus begins when he reap-

15

pears in the pages of all four Gospels with his fateful meeting with John the Baptist, whose theological function it is to baptize (symbolically to anoint) him. With this "water anointment" Jesus became, in the eyes of his followers, the "son of David," the crowned king of the Jews. Within a year this symbolic coronation was to cost him his life.

At this point, the origin of the name "Jesus Christ" can be explained. "Jesus" is Greek for the Jewish name "Joshua" and "Christ" is a Greek word meaning "anoint." Thus, "Jesus Christ" simply means "Joshua, the anointed." Whereas the pedestrian word "anoint" connotes only a mortal king, the sonorous sound of "Christ" conjures up a divine mystique.

Was Jesus aware that with his baptism he would become the central figure in a vast predestination drama? Was he the Greek hero, a tragic Sisphyus,* driven by ambition, stumbling meaninglessly through history, unaware of the fate awaiting him behind the curtain of coming events? Or was he the Jewish hero, driven by a divinity to achieve a preexistent plan, heroically pursuing the role assigned to him in spite of his awareness of the final tragedy?

After his baptism, Jesus abandoned his father's trade as a carpenter to take up a full-time career as faith healer and miracle worker. As he progressed through Galilee he gathered his disciples twelve, also known as apostles.

The faith healing of Jesus seems quaint and exotic today. We must remember, however, that in his day there were few hospitals. When families could not take care of

---

*In Greek legend, Sisyphus, founder of Corinth, was doomed by Zeus to roll a stone eternally up a slope. Each time he neared the top, the stone would slip from his hands and roll to the bottom, and the wearisome task would begin all over again.

16

their paranoids, hysterics, or epileptics, they often threw them in the streets to shift for themselves among the lame, the blind, and the halt. Except in Israel, this street scene is still common in the Middle East today.

These street people were the first patients of Jesus. As his fame as a wonder-therapist grew, audiences increased, and his public ministrations began to resemble outdoor free clinics, with the usual assortment of the sick—cripples, hysterics, and epileptics. With Jesus it was never a case of tentative diagnosis or prolonged therapy. He cured on the spot by touch or voice. In several instances he healed by long distance, merely by pronouncing that the absent individual had been cured. The Gospels record no instance of a recurrence once Jesus had effected a cure.

Emboldened by his success, Jesus returned to Nazareth to perform miracles in his hometown and to reveal what he believed to be his true identity—the messiah. It turned out to be a disaster.

All began well. He was invited to the synagogue on the Sabbath to read a portion of the Old Testament. The text was from Isaiah (61:2), and Jesus read:

> The spirit of the Lord is upon me, because he hath anointed me to preach the Gospel to the poor . . . to heal the brokenhearted . . . to preach the acceptable year of the Lord. (Luke 4:18–19).

So far so good. But then Jesus closed the Isaiah scroll and announced: "Today Scripture has been fulfilled in me." Thus he had boldly and openly announced his candidacy for messiah.

This was a mistake. "The people looked upon each other in amazement and took offense at him."

But Jesus did not stop here. He went on to inflame the people with an unkind parable, whereupon, in the words of Luke, "all in the synagogue were filled with wrath." The people of Nazareth considered throwing him down a precipice.

But Jesus escaped. On this note of disgrace, the First Act is over.

Several weeks after the curtain has gone up on the Second Act, Jesus is aimlessly wandering in Galilee and Judah, preaching and healing. But his former enthusiasm seems to be lacking.

After weeks of desultory wanderings, Jesus and his disciples came to Caesare Philippi, a Gentile city at the southern tip of Mount Hermon, a town long the favorite seat of the Greek cult-god Pan and Canaanite fertility deities. It is here in this pagan city that a revived Jesus springs to life, no longer a messianic Hamlet, dubious of his course. His family and his hometown have spurned him. Very well! He will reveal his identity to his disciples instead, and make a new start.

This, too, proves to be a fiasco. He makes known to his disciples that he is "the Christ" and that as "the Christ" he must go to Jerusalem to fulfill his destiny. It is here, too, that he states for the first time his four predictions—that he will be arrested by the Jewish priests, tried by the Romans, crucified by the Romans, and risen on the third day. But they are not impressed. As he and his small band make their way to Jerusalem, he makes two more attempts to implant the course of future events in their minds, but to no avail. In the paraphrased words of Luke, they were dense and understood him not.

While resting at Bethany, Jesus receives a message

that his friend Lazarus is ill. But when he arrives, Lazarus has been dead four days. Jesus is led to his tomb and commands him to come out. The dead man rises from death and comes out, his face and feet bound with bandages. Jesus commands the onlookers to unbind him and let him go. Now his disciples are impressed.

Will it all happen as Jesus has predicted? Will he be arrested, tried, and crucified, and will he rise on the third day? Slowly the curtain falls on Act Two as Jesus rides toward Jerusalem to keep his appointment with destiny.

When the curtain goes up on Act Three, it is the day after the Sabbath—Day One, as the Jews name the days of the week, or Palm Sunday, as the day will become known in Christian history. The narrative now proceeds swiftly as all four predictions of Jesus are to be fulfilled.

It is the day of triumph for Jesus as he rides toward the Golden Gate, one of the seven gates leading into walled Jerusalem. The crowds grow wild as he nears. The people wave palm branches at him (hence Palm Sunday) and cry "Hosanna, Son of David." He is openly acclaimed king of the Jews. Then Palm Sunday is over. The last hosanna has been shouted. All is quiet; the streets are empty.

On Monday, his second day in Jerusalem, Jesus heads for the Temple to "cleanse" it. "You have made it unto a den of thieves," he accuses the moneychangers as he overturns their coin tables and drives them out. He then sets out to preach about the new Kingdom of Heaven. Has Jesus with these actions laid the groundwork for an arrest and trial?

The third day is one of controversy. Relentlessly Jesus hammers away at his four horsemen of evil—scribes, elders, Pharisees, and Sadducees.

The fourth day, Wednesday, is one of mystery be-

19

cause there is no record of what Jesus did that day. But the evening of the fifth day is the setting for the famed "Last Supper," the Passover meal where Jesus predicts he will be betrayed by Judas.

After the meal, Jesus goes with his disciples to the Garden of Gethsemane, an orchard on the Mount of Olives outside Jerusalem, to pray. Shortly thereafter, as he has predicted, Judas betrays him, pointing him out to an arresting party consisting of an armed rabble, or a detachment of Temple police, or a band or cohort of Roman soldiers, depending upon which Gospel one reads. After a brief clash, the armed disciples take ignominious flight, and Jesus passively submits to his arrest.

Jesus is brought as a prisoner to the court of the Sanhedrin,★ or to the home of the high priest, or to Annas, the brother-in-law of the high priest—again depending upon which Gospel one reads.

With midnight begins the sixth day, Good Friday. A hearing of Jesus is held by the Jews, but it is difficult to tell just where, for each Gospel has a different version. It is also difficult to assess on just what charge Jesus is tried, because all the Gospels are vague and contradictory on this point. The most popular view is that Jesus was convicted on the charge of blasphemy and sentenced to death by the Sanhedrin, then taken for a second trial to the Roman governor of Judea, Pontius Pilate.

The nightmare for Jesus begins at daybreak, when he is taken before Pilate to be tried for treason—for having proclaimed himself king of the Jews. Pilate thinks him innocent and offers the Jews a curious choice—he will free one prisoner, either Jesus or a convicted rebel named Barabbas. The Gospels state that the Jews chose Barabbas,

★The Jewish "high court," whose functions were somewhat equivalent to those of the U.S. Supreme Court.

and Pilate sentenced Jesus to death. His first and second predictions have been fulfilled.

The Roman soldiers strip Jesus of his clothing, plait a crown of thorns for his head, spit upon him, kneel before him, shouting mockingly, "Hail, King of the Jews." After having had this Roman fun, the soldiers place a cross of wood on his back and, under a hail of jeers, lead him away to Golgotha to be crucified.

Golgotha (or Calvary, the name Luke gives it) is a steep cone of gray rock, about thirty-five feet high, flattening into a plateau at the top. Though a mile away from the place of the trial, Golgotha was still within the city limits, close to a busy street and adjacent to the wall surrounding Jerusalem. During the reign of Emperor Hadrian (117–38 A.D.), Golgotha was used by the Romans as a huge pedestal for a statue of Venus.

At the foot of the cross, the Roman soldiers roll dice for Jesus' clothes. At 9:00 A.M., Jesus is raised on the cross between two thieves (or rebels) also condemned to death. After six hours on the cross, Jesus states he is faint, and a vinegar-soaked rag on a stave is raised to his lips. He sinks into a coma and, at 3:00 P.M., expires. His third prediction has been fulfilled.

What year did that crucifixion take place? Again, depending on the Gospel of one's choice, it could have been anytime between the year 30 and 33 A.D., but popular tradition has set it at the year 30 A.D.

No sooner has Jesus seemingly expired on the cross, than Joseph of Arimathea, a secret follower of his, rushes to Pilate to request permission to take down the body so he can bury it before the Sabbath. Since it usually took three to four days to expire on the cross, Pilate, suspicious that Jesus should have died so soon, sends some soldiers to investigate.

As the two rebels crucified along with Jesus are still alive on their crosses, the soldiers, to save themselves another trip to Golgotha, break their legs.* They do not break the legs of Jesus because, seeing him lifeless, they do not deem it necessary. Suspicious, nevertheless, one soldier pierces Jesus' side with a spear. As Jesus still gives no sign of life, permission is granted to Arimathea to take down the body. It is wrapped in a linen shroud and placed in a previously prepared tomb, a huge stone rolled in front of it to seal the entrance.

When the sun goes up on the sixth day, it is Saturday, the "Day of Silence." Nothing happens.

Sunday, Easter Sunday, is the Day of Resurrection.

Three women—Mary Magdalene and two companions—are the first to learn of this resurrection. Coming to the tomb, they find the stone rolled away and the body of Jesus gone. An angel (or two, or three, depending on the Gospel one reads) informs them Jesus has risen.

Has the fourth prediction been fulfilled?

A few days later, Jesus himself appears before his disciples to remind them that he has risen and that all his prophecies and predictions have been fulfilled. The curtain now comes down on the Third Act of this salvation drama, heralding the coming two millennia of Christianity.

For 1700 years, the concept of Jesus as the son of God was the only one taught in all Christendom. The penalty for entertaining any other view was usually painful death. Not until the eighteenth century, with the Age of Rationalism, did men dare to question this version. A new theological discipline was born, that of higher biblical

---

*The reason for this seemingly irrational action will be discussed in another chapter.

criticism, a historical examination of the Old and New Testaments. The moment scholars dared to examine Gospel events critically, the evangelists' accounts began to shatter, as new facts placed old assumptions in jeopardy.

Let us now join the scholars of this new school of higher biblical criticism in their quest for the historical Jesus.

Chapter 3

Four Saints in a Fight for the Gospel Truth

The question of a historical Jesus was not raised until after the Reformation. Even Martin Luther sided with the popes in their view that there was no need to analyze either the Old or New Testaments. "If a difficulty arises in regard to Scripture," wrote Luther, "we must just leave it alone."

Among the first to be sentenced to death for searching for a historical Jesus was, interestingly enough, not a Catholic burned by the Church but a Protestant burned by a renowned Reformation leader. In 1553, the Spanish Protestant theologian Michael Servetius (born 1511) was burned at the stake in Geneva on the orders of John Calvin himself. Servetius's crime was a heinous one. He not only had denied the divinity of Jesus but had reduced him to a mere prophet. His views were based mostly on guesswork, however, not on a systematic study of the Gospels.

A more critical school of Bible study began in the early eighteenth century with English deists like John Toland (1670–1722) and Thomas Woolston (1670–1730). These deists, like Servetius, not only looked upon Jesus as a mere prophet, but they also denied the miraculous nature of the miracles, substituting rational explanations for presumed divine manifestations. So, for instance, they held that Jesus did not raise people from the dead but had merely brought them out of a coma resembling death. Jesus, they explained, had walked not upon the Sea of Galilee but along the shore, for with the fog—and the grog the disciples might have imbibed—they merely thought he was walking on the water.

The French deists, on the other hand, rejected the miracles as barefaced inventions or as plain fraud. Voltaire acknowledged Jesus might have been a prophet, but Rousseau dismissed him as a mere Hebrew sage.

Modern biblical criticism based on historical research did not begin until the mid-eighteenth century in Germany. For about a century (1750–1850), the overwhelming number of scholars in search of the historical Jesus, however, did not start out searching solely for the historical truth. Underneath their scholarship smoldered a hatred of Catholicism and a resentment toward Christianity because it paid homage to a Jew. Many of them therefore felt compelled to topple the crown of glory the Church had placed on the head of Jesus and replace it with Pilate's crown of thorns, which, in their view, was a more fitting headgear for a Jew. The paradox was, as one scholar expressed it, "that the greatest attempts to write the life of Jesus have been written with hate."[*]

So, for instance, Albert Schweitzer, renowned author

[*] F. C. Burkitt, Preface to Albert Schweitzer's *The Quest of the Historical Jesus*. Macmillan, New York, 1961.

of *The Quest of the Historical Jesus,* says of Bruno Bauer, one of those early German Protestant Jesus-haters: "He [Bruno Bauer] felt nothing but contempt for the theologians and took fiendish joy in exposing their pseudo-history. Bauer not only hates theologians but Christianity." Of Herman Reimarus, another of these German de-mythologizers, Schweitzer wrote: "Seldom has there been hate so eloquent, so lofty of scorn."

Typical of these German debunkers of Jesus and Christianity was Eduard von Hartmann, who accused Jesus of "Semitic harshness." Jesus, said von Hartmann, "despises work, property, and the duties of family life. At heart he was a fanatic. He hates and despises the world and everything it contains."

Faith thus played little part in the work of these German scholars, who considered themselves free from any responsibility to Christianity. As they stripped away everything noble in Christianity—the Annunciation, the Magnificat, the Baptism, the Transfiguration, the Last Supper, the Resurrection—they proclaimed that this stripped residue was the true Christianity they admired. One is reminded of Freud's answer to Jung when the latter declared he admired psychoanalytic theory after he had bolted from it. "If he does not believe in my theory of dreams," was Freud's reply, "if he does not believe in my theory of infantile sexuality, and if he does not believe in the death instinct, what's left to admire?"

Psychologists are not surprised to find that many of these German scholars were also anti-Semites. Did these debunking theologians in fact also mulch the soil for the coming anti-Semitism of the Nazis?

History says "Yes." In the same way that Nietzsche's Superman was used as a prototype for the Nazi mass murderers, so, too, the derogation of Jesus was used as a prototype for the Nazi war against Christianity. Among the first scholars to perceive this relationship was the Russian existentialist theologian Nikolai Berdayev, who wrote: "The fact that German anti-Semitism evolved into anti-Christianity must be considered a significant symptom."* Yet, this basic Nazi anti-Christianity is almost totally overlooked by many historians.

In the Nazi view, Christianity represented a danger because it weakened the Aryan strain of blood among Germans through the indiscriminate baptism of alien races into that religion. The Nazis held that Christianity had been betrayed by the Jew Paul; they contended that Christian churches were a sham and a fraud and that the Catholic Church was the most dangerous of all because it was both "Jewish and international."

Nevertheless, despite their hatred of Christianity, these eighteenth-century theologians were scrupulously honest in their scholarship. Not for a moment, in spite of their anti-Jesus bias, did they accept the Gospel versions of the culpability of the Jews in the crucifixion as a historical fact, dismissing these accounts as fraudulent. To a man they agreed that the crucifixion was strictly a Roman affair.

Three theologians represent the main currents of this new school of higher biblical criticism. They are Herman Samuel Reimarus (1694–1768), a German Protestant Orientologist who prudently printed only "safe monographs" about Jesus during his life, leaving his controversial material to be published after his death; Joseph Ernest Renan (1823–92), a French Catholic Orientologist who wrote the first popular life of Jesus with such elan that it swept many of its readers into the main-

---

*Berdayev, *Christianity and Anti-Semitism.*

stream of unbelief; and William Wrede (1850–1907), a German Protestant philosopher and skeptic who dismissed the writings of all theologians as sheer nonsense.

Reimarus was a trailblazer, probably the greatest of all German theologians in the century from 1700 to 1800. If those who flourished after him wrote great classic works, they were only variations on the Reimarus theme.

Reimarus was born and buried in obscurity in Hamburg. With the publication of his monograph *The Goal of Jesus and His Disciples*, a theological hurricane of denunciations broke loose. Fortunately for him he had died ten years before its publication in 1778. Had he been alive, the explosion it caused would have blown him into the Kingdom Come where he already was.

According to Reimarus, primitive Christianity grew not only out of the teachings of Jesus, but also from subsequent events that added new ideas not contained in his preachings. Baptism and the Last Supper, he said, were not instituted by Jesus but created by the early Church on the basis of its assumptions about him.

Placing Jesus in the historical setting, Reimarus essentially came up with three views—Jesus as a Jew, Jesus as a rebel, and the disciples as "plotters" who engineered the resurrection.

Jesus saw his messiahship in a purely Jewish sense, says Reimarus, not as a literal son of God but as the son of man. He was therefore a political leader set to break the hold of Roman domination. Having failed, he paid the penalty—death by crucifixion.

To explain the resurrection, Reimarus held it was the disciples who stole the body from the tomb where it had been placed and then spread the word that Jesus had been resurrected.

Interestingly enough, this idea was not original with

Reimarus. Fifteen hundred years before, the renowned Church Father, Tertillian (circa 160–230), talking of the Second Coming of Jesus, wrote: "This is he whom his disciples have stolen away secretly, that it may be said he is risen."★

Quite different from Reimarus was Ernest Renan, who hid his anticlerical fist in a glove of polished prose. After having been seduced by the writings of the German theologians, he quit the seminary he was attending and, like Reimarus, chose a career in Orientology (Middle Eastern Studies). All hell broke loose upon the publication of his book *The Life of Jesus* in 1863 in Paris. The Pope placed it on the Index of banned books, but to no avail; the book made Jesus a fashionable conversation piece in the salons of the rich. The Church did, however, succeed in driving Renan out of his professorship into an obscurity from which he was not rescued until after his death. He was buried in the Pantheon in Paris, and history subsequently crowned him with fame.

Renan's *The Life of Jesus* was a brilliant work that reads like fiction. Some even thought of it as a "Fifth Gospel." He had the ability to infuriate the Church and charm his readers with the same phrase. Though Renan did not hold either Jesus or the Church up to ridicule, he was scornful of all theological views. He stripped the life of Jesus bare of all miracles—ascribing them to fraud, deceit, or natural causes. So, for instance, Renan held that Lazarus had staged a resurrection of himself in order to further the career of Jesus by deceiving him into believing that it had been due to his own divine powers. With his smiling skepticism, Renan had demolished the structure of pure faith, and nothing could save him now from the

★As quoted by Hugh J. Schonfield in *The Passover Plot*. Hutchinson, London, 1965.

30

fury of the Church. "With friends like this, who needs enemies," the Church might well have thought as it banned the book.

Continuing on the path blazed by Reimarus and his fellow travelers was William Wrede, professor of philosophy at the University of Breslau. With his monumental work *The Messianic Secret in the Gospels*, the wrath of Wrede compelled the theologians to give battle. "The readers of Wrede cannot help but feel that no quarter is given," wrote Albert Schweitzer.

Wrede held that not a single assertion by theologians need be accepted unless first proven by them. The Gospels, he asserted, were not historical works but literary inventions. It was, therefore, up to the theologians to prove them accurate before a historian needed to take them seriously. Either the Gospels are historical, he said, in which case there was no need to explain away the plain meaning of the text, or else they were unhistorical, in which case they should be dismissed.

The demythologizing scholars from Reimarus to Wrede had a terrifying impact on the theology of the times. Fundamentalist theologians were fearful of what these writings might do to the concept of Jesus as the messiah and to Christianity itself. When Albert Schweitzer wrote that "We must be prepared to find that the knowledge and personality of Jesus will not be a help but perhaps even an offense to religion," his words sent a chill down ecclesiastic spines.*

In spite of its attack on Church dogma, Renan's *The Life of Jesus* was a turning point in the development of biblical criticism. It blunted the brutal attacks by the German Protestant scholars on the Church and Christianity

*Schweitzer, *The Quest of the Historical Jesus*.

and paved the way for a new school of more liberal and tolerant biblical scholars—Protestants, Catholics, and even Jews.* Unlike the Germans, these new thinkers were less antagonistic to religion. Though they all stood on the shoulders of the German theologians, benefiting from their Teutonic spadework, the new liberal scholars were not so much interested in vilifying Jesus and debunking Christianity as they were in trying to solve specific puzzles in the life and death of Jesus. Both schools, however, found the Gospel accounts of the arrest, trial, crucifixion, and resurrection unhistorical.

The liberals echoed the radicals by asking the same questions: Why did the Jews arrest Jesus? There seemed to be no logical or historical reason for it. Was it essential for Judas to betray Jesus, and if so, why? As described in the contradictory Gospel accounts, the incident seemed trivial, unnecessary, and contrived.

More questions: Why would Pilate hold a second trial of Jesus if the Sanhedrin had already convicted him? The Gospel explanations collapse under the pressure of historical evidence. And why did the evangelists switch the original charge against Jesus from blasphemy against the Jewish religion to treason against Rome when Jesus was brought before Pilate? Again, the explanations offered in the Gospels are contrary to those provided by history.

And further questions: What is the true identity of Barabbas? What really happened at the cross on Golgotha? Who were the two "thieves" crucified with Jesus? History tells us the Romans did not crucify thieves.

To find the answers to these and other related puzzles, the scholars placed the evangelists in the witness box and subjected them to a rigorous cross-examination. Amazing

---

* As a rule Jewish scholars have stayed out of this fracas, feeling it essentially is a Christian family affair.

discrepancies in the testimony emerged almost immediately.

A most glaring one was that the Jesus of the synoptic Gospels did not seem to be the same Jesus as in John's. The "synoptic" Jesus was arrested by the Jews on the fifteenth day of Nisan, a Friday, sentenced to death at night by the Sanhedrin, taken to Pilate at daybreak, sentenced to death a second time by the Romans, raised to the cross at nine in the morning, where he died at three in the afternoon.

In John's Gospel, on the other hand, Jesus was arrested on the fourteenth day of Nisan, not the fifteenth, on a Thursday not a Friday, by the Romans not by the Jews. In John's Gospel, Jesus was not tried by the Jews or sentenced to death by them. Only the Romans held a trial, and only the Romans sentenced him to death. In John's Gospel, Jesus was raised to the cross in the afternoon, not in the morning, and he died late in the evening, not at three in the afternoon.

Why such a difference in dates, times, and procedures? Both views can't be right. One is wrong. Which Gospel should one believe? cynical scholars ask. In the heat of this scholarly skepticism, the theological solder, which for eighteen centuries had held the Gospel structure together, melted, and the edifice collapsed.

The Gospel accounts of the arrest and two trials of Jesus fared especially badly under the impact of the cross-examination. They are so full of discrepancies and inaccuracies that scholars no longer take them seriously as historical accounts but view them rather as frail memory enriched with faith.

This in essence is the consolidated story of the synoptic evangelists of the arrest and trial of Jesus. He was arrested by a rabble of scribes, priests, and elders, armed with swords and clubs. The mob dragged Jesus to the palace of the high priest (or to the Sanhedrin, depending on which Gospel one reads) who sent searchers into the night to find some prevaricators to give false witness against him. The high priest asked Jesus, "Are you the Christ, the son of the Blessed?" When Jesus answered, "Yes," the high priest tore his mantle and cried, "You have heard this blasphemy." Whereupon Jesus, according to these synoptic accounts, was condemned to death, spat upon, beaten, and hauled to Pontius Pilate at daybreak for a confirmation of the death sentence.

This synoptic Gospel account of the arrest and trial of Jesus by the Jews is in fact so absurd that even the Dominican scholar Father Roland de Vaux, in his monumental study, *Ancient Israel, Its Life and Institutions*, states that the trial as portrayed in the Gospels could not have happened according to either Jewish or Roman law.

In Jewish law, scholars point out, no one could be arrested at night. It was illegal to hold court proceedings after sundown on the eve of the Sabbath or a festival. The Great Sanhedrin could convene only in the Chamber of the Hewn Stones, never in the palace of the high priest or any other dwelling. The Sanhedrin could not initiate an arrest any more than the United States Supreme Court can, nor could anyone be tried unless two witnesses had first sworn out charges against the accused. As there was no prosecuting attorney in those days, the accusing witnesses had to state the nature of the offense in the presence of the accused, who had a right to call witnesses in his own behalf. The court then examined and cross-examined the accused, the accusers, and the defense witnesses.

John is more in accord with the view of Father Roland de Vaux than with his contemporaries Mark, Matthew, and Luke. According to John's Gospel, the synoptic evangelists did not know what they were talking about. John avers that it was not a mob of scribes and elders armed with clubs who arrested Jesus, but a cohort* of Roman soldiers with swords, accompanied by some Jewish police officers. According to John, the Jews never sentenced Jesus to death. Instead, John describes a curious triple play wherein Jesus was taken successively from Annas** to Caiaphas† to Pilate, who sentenced him to the cross. It is a question of believing either John or the synoptics. One version excludes the other, and only one side could be telling it as it was.

By arranging the Four Gospels into four parallel columns in chronological sequence—from Mark in 70 to Matthew in 85 to Luke in 90 to John in 110 A.D.—to compare how the evangelists treated the same event in their respective Gospels, the scholars noted a fascinating escalation in hyperbole. As time went by, with each successive evangelist, the miracles became more miraculous, the vilification of the Jews more intensified, the guilt of the Jews obsessively expanded, the crucifixion enriched with ever more detail, and the resurrection attested to by

---

*Most Protestant translations of the Bible, including the King James, use the word "band" or "group," implying a smaller force than a cohort. However, the *Douay Bible* (1582–1609), the authorized Catholic translation, and the Jerusalem Bible (1966) do use "cohort" for the simple reason that this is the word St. Jerome used in his Vulgate, first authorized Latin translation (385–405). That, too, was the word John himself used in composing his Gospel—the Greek word *speira* meaning "cohort." The editors of both the *Revised Version* and *The Abingdon Bible Commentary* concur with the Vulgate, the Douay, and the Jerusalem Bible that John wrote "a cohort" and not "a band."

**The brother-in-law of the high priest.

†The high priest.

35

an ever-increasing number of angels and personal appearances by Jesus before his disciples—from none in the original Mark to three in John.*

The progressive vilification of the Jews is of special interest. From Gospel to Gospel, in chronological order, it becomes increasingly bitter as Jews refuse to join Christianity while pagan converts swell its ranks. In Mark the main attack is centered on some scribes, elders, and Pharisees. Matthew and Luke enlarge this field of hate by throwing in all scribes, elders, Pharisees, and Sadducees. By the time this hate-wave reaches John, it has spread to all Jews.

Some scholars have a fascinating explanation for this unseemly abuse of the people of Jesus. Though the method is ethically questionable, they point out that politically it was sound strategy. We must recall, they remind us, that by 70 A.D., the Romans despised and feared the Christians as subversives. Mark realized it would be dangerous to make the Romans the villains in this drama, and pragmatically chose the Jews for this role. Having rapacious Pilate defend Jesus was a stroke of genius. It showed the Romans that their own procurator thought well of the Christians because their leader had cooperated with the Empire by advising the Jews to "render unto Caesar what is Caesar's." It was such an excellent ploy that each successive evangelist seized upon it, each in turn further embellishing Jewish villainy while extolling Pilate's saintliness.

The problem arises: Why did not the evangelists get their stories straight and compare notes to avoid at least the

---

*The question of the original versus the traditional Gospel of Mark will be discussed in another chapter.

most embarrassing contradictions? The solution comes only with hindsight. When the evangelists wrote, they had no idea that within a few centuries their Gospels would be immortalized into a "New Testament." When they wrote, each Gospel was an independent document, each circulating in separate corners of the vast Roman Empire.

The evangelists had to slant their Gospels to meet local challenges. Therefore it did not matter if their stories did not match, as long as they solved their respective problems. In Rome, where Mark wrote his Gospel, he had headaches with the Romans, who threw Christians to the lions. In Alexandria, Matthew had his hands full with the Jews, who, being the largest segment in the city, gave him not only the most trouble but also the largest number of converts. Luke in Antioch and John in Ephesus wrote for the Christians who were former pagans and did not know a Pharisee from a Viking.

The early Church was fully aware of these contradictions and at one time (in the late second century) did consider weaving the Four Gospels into one, with all inconsistencies eliminated. However, this plan was soon abandoned as a hopeless task. The distinctive and incomparable literary style of each evangelist could be neither matched nor submerged. The Church wisely decided to brave the inconsistencies of four separate literary gems rather than be stuck with one dull document no one would read. For seventeen centuries the Church had little problem with this, until the German Protestant theologians came along and spoiled the serenity.

As the scholars continued to subject the Gospels to ever-greater in-depth analysis, they noted that just as the portrait of Jesus as the son of God had been painted by theologians with selected sentences from the Gospels, so they too could create other portraits of Jesus with different sets of sentences from the same Gospels. Thus the scholars came up with six additional faces, or portraits, of Jesus, all consonant with the testimony of the evangelists.

But if all seven portraits are drawn with different sets of sentences from the same Four Gospels, which portrait represents the true Jesus? To prove their respective theories, the scholars set out on a journey into archaeology and history to test which Gospel assertions were embedded in mere faith and which were encrusted with solid facts. It was felt that the portrait painted with the greatest number of factual events would represent the most historical Jesus.

Of special interest to these scholars were the four enigmatic predictions made by Jesus. They probed first for the reasons behind the predictions, then for how they were fulfilled. As the scholars sketched their divergent views, the function of these predictions and the mechanism for their fulfillment were brought to light.

Brilliant though these scholars were, they did not come up with the same conclusions as to who the real Jesus might be. Each school beheld a different view. They resembled pagan priests divining different interpretations from the quivering entrails of the same sacrificial animal. Paradoxically, the more facts they uncovered, the more elusive became the historical Jesus. Although this scholarly quest may be viewed as a search for a secular grail, it did, however, take Jesus out of the realm of theology and place him firmly in the world of politics and history.

Let us now visit the Gospel gallery where hang our seven portraits of Jesus and, with the scholars, unveil the second, that of Jesus as a Jew, the messiah as the son of man.

PART TWO

What the Search for the Historical Jesus Revealed

Chapter 4

The Jewish Connection

A s we shift the lens of history from "Jesus as a Christian" to "Jesus as a Jew," a fascinating change in emphasis takes place. The story proceeds no longer as a Christian predestination drama but becomes a Jewish existentialist tragedy. In this scenario, Jesus is not the Christian "son of God" at the center of the action. He is the self-proclaimed Jewish messiah, the "son of man," waiting offstage in the wings of future history.

The moment the curtain goes up on the presentation of Jesus as a Jew, the dilemma of the synoptic evangelists becomes clear. Though the Gospel writers lived outside Palestine, in the pagan world of the Roman Empire, everything they wrote had to take place in a Jewish milieu and in consonance with the Old Testament. The life and death of Jesus had to conform to that document; the Jesus drama had to be modeled on a "Jewish plan," or Jesus would not be credible. Only the Old Testament could give him the authenticity claimed for him.

Even a cursory reading of the Gospels reveals how Jewish Jesus had to be in order to be a legitimate candidate for messiahship. The Old Testament prophets state that the future messiah must be a descendant of King David; the evangelists state that Jesus is of Davidic descent. The Old Testament proclaims the Jews are the Chosen People; the Gospels proclaim Jesus is the "chosen son." The Jews wandered for forty years in the wilderness; Jesus wanders for forty days in the desert. Moses received the Covenant—the Torah—on Mount Sinai; Jesus receives his symbolic "new covenant"—that is, his transfiguration—on Mount Hermon. The Jews were divided into twelve tribes; Jesus selects twelve disciples

There is also an element of compulsive one-upmanship in the constant introduction of Jewish prototypes into the life of Jesus. Whatever the Jewish patriarchs and prophets do, Jesus has to do it better. Elisha heals a leper by command; Jesus heals ten by thought. Elijah ascends to heaven in a chariot; Jesus ascends to heaven to sit at the right hand of God. Moses divides the Red Sea and walks through it; Jesus walks on the water of the Sea of Galilee. When Moses goes up Mount Sinai, his face shines; when Jesus goes up Mount Hermon, not only his face but even his garments shine.

In the Old Testament, God puts family ahead of serving Him; Jesus puts service to himself ahead of the family. So, for instance, when God asks Elisha to serve Him, Elisha asks God for permission to first say good-bye to his parents and receives it. When one of Jesus' disciples asks for permission to bury his father before joining him, Jesus refuses that request by replying, "Let the dead bury their dead." Moses goes to God to receive his powers and works through God. Jesus never goes to God to receive his powers; he merely states that he has been given them by God and exercises them at his own will.

Ironically, what many Christians consider most Christian in Jesus is actually Jewish. If one were to ask a Christian which passages in the Gospels are "most Christian," the answer probably would be the Beatitudes* and the Lord's Prayer. These two magnificent word cantatas by Jesus are indeed beautiful, moving sermons; yet nothing could be more Jewish. And for a very good reason —almost all of their content and wording comes from the Old Testament.

Surely one would think that the famed Beatitude, "Blessed are the meek for they shall inherit the earth," is purely Christian. Not at all. It is Jewish to the core. It is from Psalm 37:11, in which King David sings to the Lord: "The meek shall possess and delight themselves in abundant prosperity."

The same holds true for these Beatitudes: "Blessed are the pure in heart, for they shall see God." King David said that first in Psalm 24, one thousand years before— "He who has a pure heart . . . will receive blessing from the Lord."

"Blessed are they that hunger after righteousness, for they shall be filled," says Jesus. This time he is paraphrasing Isaiah (Chapter 55), where God bids those thirsting after righteousness to come to Him. Isaiah is also the source for the Beatitude, "Blessed are they that mourn, for they shall be comforted." It is based on verses in Chapter 61, where Isaiah proclaims, "the Lord has anointed me to bring good tidings to the afflicted . . . to comfort all who mourn."

---

*Matthew 5:3–12; Luke 6:20–23.

The evangelists did not originate these Beatitudes and then attribute them to Jesus. Jesus the Jew did say them. He quoted or paraphrased these Beatitudes as part of the glory and beauty of the Old Testament. His audiences, like him, being Jewish, did not need quotation marks; they knew the sources without being told.

The Lord's Prayer, too, touches heart and mind. But every sentence in it can be traced to the Old Testament. The genius of Jesus was in his rephrasing and rearranging material from the Old Testament into a separate prayer. But the ideas in that prayer are all authentically Jewish, originating in the Jewish past and finding their first written expression in the Old Testament.

The Gospels tell the story of a lawyer mocking Jesus with the question, "What should I do to inherit eternal life?" Jesus answers him with a double-barreled Jewish answer: "Thou shalt love thy God with all thy strength and with all thy mind, and love thy neighbor as thyself." The first part is from Deuteronomy (6:4), the second from Leviticus (19:18).

But, one may argue, if Jesus is so Jewish, why did he have all those arguments with scribes, priests, and Pharisees? Today, however, few Christians pay heed to these disputations; in fact they tend to side with the Pharisee view.

Let us examine two of these tempests in Pharisee teacups—the disputations about washing one's hands before sitting down to eat, and healing on the Sabbath.

Jesus fulminates at the Pharisee tradition of washing one's hands before sitting down to eat, defending his disciples for not doing so. Perhaps the disciples were just plain uncouth. Civilization has already made its judgment—it is better to wash one's hands before a meal than to eat with dirty ones.

Equally pointless is the brouhaha about Jesus' healing on the Sabbath. Jewish law does not prohibit saving a life on the Sabbath; it merely declares that ordinary healing involving no risk to life should be deferred, like other manual work. What the Pharisees said was simply that Jesus could have healed lepers and epileptics on the day after the Sabbath.

This Pharisee viewpoint has already been accepted by Christianity. Surgery not involving life and death, for instance, is not performed on Sunday, but held over until Monday. However, what Jesus did would not have been considered against the Sabbath laws anyway, because he healed not by work but by thought and voice. According to Mosaic Law, one can think and talk as much as one wants to on the Sabbath, and healing someone in the process is not a sin but could in fact be considered a *mitzvah*—a good deed.

Reading the Gospels, one gets the impression that the Jews were a fossilized people among whom spiteful Pharisees, Sadducees, scribes, and elders ran amok, with nothing better to do than pick quarrels with Jesus and plot against his life. Quite the contrary. Jerusalem at that time was a lively, cosmopolitan metropolis where twenty-four different religious sects rubbed elbows and dogmas, one such sect being the Jewish followers of Jesus. In the days of Jesus, the Temple was not the only center of religious life; in fact, it was a slowly disappearing one. There were already over twenty synagogues in Jerusalem fighting the Temple for membership.

To understand what happened historically, it is important to place Jesus in the real world.

Let us journey beyond theology and see what history has to say about the Jewish Jesus, and recapitulate the events of the fateful days from Palm Sunday to the day of resurrection, which embody the time span of his four predictions. This time, however, let us view these events in situ, to see how they appeared to the people in Jerusalem at the time they happened.

Five enigmatic milestones line the path Jesus took from the Golden Gate to Golgotha. If we can penetrate the secret each hides, we can perceive Jesus in a new historical perspective. These five crucial milestones are: The entry into Jerusalem; the cleansing of the Temple; the Jewish charges against Jesus; the Roman trial; and, finally, the crucifixion itself.

Until his entry into Jerusalem, Jews and Romans had little cause to regard Jesus as anything more than another harmless religious preacher, no threat to the Roman state or Jewish religion. To the Jews, until that fateful arrival in Jerusalem, Jesus was an ordinary, itinerant rabbi wandering through the country, preaching, healing, and performing wonders.

Pontius Pilate might even have viewed Jesus as a friend of Rome, for everything he had said until then seemed to fit right in with what an occupying governor would want his subjects to say and do. "Resist no evil," preached Jesus. That suited the Romans just fine. "Whosoever shall smite you on the right cheek, turn him the other also," taught Jesus. This struck a responsive chord among the Romans, who loved nothing better than to have such docile Jews under their rule.

And there were such adages by Jesus as "Bless them that curse you," and "Do good to them that hate you." All such sentiments were tailor-made for an occupying power and could not have been better expressed in an official Roman handbook for vanquished nations on how to behave toward the conqueror.

The entry of Jesus into Jerusalem was the turning

point in his messianic career. Jesus knew that from the moment he was hailed by the people as the son of David, as a liberator, he would be a marked man, a traitor in Roman eyes. He also knew that with that action he had not only committed treason against Rome but had also placed the Jewish rulers on the horns of a terrible dilemma. Was he setting the stage for the fulfillment of his first two predictions?

The Jewish leaders, aware that Jesus had committed treason against Rome by allowing himself to be proclaimed king, had to resolve this dilemma. What should they do? Should they arrest Jesus and turn him over to the Romans to prevent reprisals against the entire Jewish nation? But to turn in a Jew to the hated Romans was as abhorrent to the Jews as turning in a freedom fighter to the hated Nazis during World War II was to the Danes and Norwegians. The evangelists state that dilemma succinctly—should they (the Jewish leaders) "let one man die or an entire nation perish"?

Or should they spirit Jesus away, out of reach of the Romans? But this action was too fraught with danger. It could precipitate a crisis that would lead to thousands of crucified Jews lining the road from Caesaria to Jerusalem.

Or perhaps they could restrain Jesus from his collision course with the Romans by arresting him, talking some sense into him, and then pacifying the Romans by explaining it was all a Passover prank, a lot of sound and fury signifying nothing politically.

Prudently, the Jews decided to wait. They took no action, hoping nothing would happen and that they would have a peaceful Passover the coming weekend.

It seemed like a good decision. The crowds went home. Night fell. All was peaceful. The Romans too withheld action to see if the incident at the Golden Gate was perhaps but an isolated event rather than the first step in a revolt. Maybe the entire episode of Jesus' riding into Jerusalem on the colt of an ass and being hailed as a messiah by some religious zealots was nothing more than another example of Jewish emotionalism. This interpretation fits all the facts presented by the Gospels.

We now reach the second milestone. On the following day Jesus made his next move, the "cleansing of the Temple." Scholars are puzzled by this episode. What did Jesus hope to accomplish with his action? Did he want to reform the priesthood? Was he against sacrifice? The answer to both questions is "No."

The prophets had begun the reformation of the Temple cult eight hundred years before Jesus. When he appeared on the scene, the power of the Temple priesthood had already been challenged. There existed by this time two Judaisms side by side—one Sadducee, the other Pharisee—in the same way two Christianities exist side by side today—one Catholic, the other Protestant.

Sadducee Judaism was the cult of Temple and sacrifice attended to by priests. Pharisee Judaism was a revolt against that practice. The Pharisees substituted synagogues for Temple, prayer for sacrifice, and rabbis for priests, much in the same manner the Protestants substituted ministers for priests, congregational authority for Vatican authority, and everyday speech for Latin in prayers.

It was a long-established custom in the days of Jesus to sell sacrificial doves, sheep, and oxen outside the Temple sanctuary. Because pilgrims came from many lands to offer their sacrifices, it was customary for the vendors to make change from one currency to another. With his "cleansing of the Temple," Jesus had a very modest aim—not to do away with sacrifice and priesthood, but to end the practice of handling money on Temple grounds.

When Jesus arrived at the Temple, he overturned the tables of the moneychangers. Curiously, the Jews did not arrest him as a disturber of the peace. For the next three days, Jesus went to the Temple where, unopposed, he denounced both the Pharisees and the Sadducees in the most harsh and abusive language.

In Matthew's "Woe to you" chapter (23) the Jews are given the full litany of vilification—hypocrites, vipers, dogs, liars, serpents. Matthew even accuses the Jews of having killed some of their prophets.

History, however, testifies to the fact that not a single prophet was ever killed by the Jews, remarkable indeed when one considers that in an age of priesthood the prophets dared to thunder that vain sacrifices were an abomination unto God. What would have happened in the Middle Ages had Cardinals dared denounce the veneration of statues of Jesus as idolatry? One need not wonder. History has already rendered its verdict. Gibbon★ records that in the first three centuries after the Christian takeover of the Roman Empire (380 A.D.), the Christians killed in assorted gruesome ways more fellow Christians suspected of heresy than the Romans had in the previous three centuries.

It was, in fact, safer to be a Christian in Jerusalem in the first century A.D. than it was to be a Christian fifteen centuries later in Medieval Europe. During the Thirty Years War (1618–48) Catholics and Protestants killed each other by the hundreds of thousands in the name of Jesus. No Christian in the days of the Apostolic Church in Jerusalem (31–70 A.D.) ever experienced the horrors of a

★Gibbon, *The Decline and Fall of the Roman Empire*. Harcourt Brace, New York, 1960.

bloodbath like that of St. Bartholomew's Night (1572 A.D.), when Catholics within twelve hours slew thirty thousand Huguenots (French Protestants) in their beds. And history does not let us forget the autos-da-fé, which lit up the Christian sky for three centuries.

Thus, judged against history, the tolerance of the Jews toward the Christian sect was most remarkable.

Nothing pejorative has been intended by these examples. In the words of Robert Burns, "Oh, wad some pow'r the giftie gie us, To see oursels as others see us." We must have the tolerance to view events as they appeared to people in bygone days. In rejecting Jesus in the first century A.D., the Jews were no different from the Christians who rejected Allah and Mohammed in the seventh century A.D., when the new religion of Islam was born.

Despite his provocative actions and words, Jesus was not arrested by the Jews. He was not burned or flayed or quartered—the Christian punishment for heretical utterances; nor was he stoned to death—the Jewish punishment for blasphemy in those days. In fact, Jesus was not arrested until Friday, midnight, the sixth day after his entry into Jerusalem. But why then? And by whom? Here lies our third enigmatic milestone—the Jewish charges against Jesus.

We have already examined the contradictions inherent in the accounts of the synoptic evangelists, who claim that Jesus was arrested by the Jews, taken to the Sanhedrin, and sentenced to death. John denies this, asserting that Jesus was arrested by a Roman cohort, never tried by the Jews or sentenced to death by them.

Why does John contradict Mark, Matthew, and Luke? If John is right in stating that no charges were pressed against Jesus by the Jews, why then was he arrested? If the synoptics are correct in stating that Jesus was condemned to death by the Jews, of what crime was he presumed to be guilty?

The synoptic evangelists allege that Jesus was accused of blasphemy and sentenced to death after conviction on that charge. Scholars are puzzled by this. Blasphemy, according to Jewish law, could be committed only by cursing God and pronouncing His name. Since Jesus was not accused of either of these infractions, he could not have been brought up on that charge.

Yet, the trial of Jesus is not a myth. It was not the invention of the evangelists. Though they may be blind to history, though they may be motivated by theology, though they may err in detail after detail, nevertheless the Gospel writers are dealing with historical fact. The question is not whether Jesus was arrested and tried, and condemned to death. He was. The question is, by whom? With this question we arrive at the fourth milestone—the Roman trial.

If we concentrate on those points on which Mark, Matthew, and Luke agree, a new cluster of facts emerges. Though the synoptic evangelists agree that Jesus was sentenced to death by the Jews for a religious crime, a switch takes place. Instead of being put to death by the Jews for this alleged religious crime of blasphemy, as one would expect, Jesus is instead executed by the Romans for a political crime. This brings up two questions: Why did the Jews not execute Jesus themselves, if he was guilty? And why this sudden switch from blasphemy against the Jews to treason against the Romans?

The first question placed the evangelists in a dilemma, but they came up with an ingenious answer. The Jews, they said, had to get permission from the Romans to impose the death sentence.

51

This explanation runs into a dead end. Not only is there no historical evidence for it, but there is considerable evidence against it. The New Testament itself gives two examples to the contrary. When the apostle Stephen was found guilty of blasphemy, he was stoned to death by the Jews without permission from the Romans. And James, one of the twelve disciples, was also executed without any previous clearance from the Romans.

As for the second question—why the switch from blasphemy to treason—the answer is, many scholars say, that there never were two trials, only one. Most historians today believe Jesus was never tried by the Jews for blasphemy or any other charge. They hold that it was only the Romans who held a trial of Jesus, condemning him to death because they considered him a traitor to Rome.

Here is the view of Maurice Goguel, famed French theologian: "In reality Jesus was not tried by the Sanhedrin. At the moment Jesus appeared before the high priest, he was not a prisoner of the Jews, but a prisoner of Pilate. . . . Jesus was taken before the Jewish authorities because the procurator wished it."

Oscar Cullman, another eminent historian, has this to say: "The trial and conviction of Jesus are the affair of the Romans only. . . . The hearing before the high priest was not a regular session of the Sanhedrin. . . . These proceedings . . . did not have the character of a trial, but of an unofficial investigation by the authorities, from which ensued the accusation before the Romans."

And the French theologian Charles Guignebert states: "The probability is that the Nazarene was arrested by the Roman police, judged and condemned by the Roman procurator."

But how can these opinions by scholars be reconciled with the exact opposite statements of the evangelists?

How can this mystery of two trials be solved? Elementary, says a new biblical Sherlock Holmes, Dr. Haim Cohn, a former justice of the Supreme Court of Israel, and an expert on ancient Roman and Israelite law. Dr. Cohn has synthesized the findings of modern biblical scholarship into an original and highly readable work entitled *The Trial and Death of Jesus.*

Under Roman law in the days of occupied Judea, he writes, the Jews had full jurisdiction over all religious crimes. If, however, a political crime—an offense against Roman occupation—had been committed, then the Romans and not the Jews had jurisdiction. Thus, if Jesus had committed blasphemy, a religious crime, the Romans would have been unconcerned, and the Jews themselves would have executed him, as was done in the cases of Stephen and James. But if Jesus had committed a political crime, the Romans would demand, as they did, that the Jews hand Jesus over to them for trial, as was done.

After analyzing the Gospel accounts in the light of present-day knowledge of Roman and Jewish law, there is no doubt that it was the Romans who wanted the arrest of Jesus, says Justice Cohn. Does it not seem more probable, he asks, that the Romans were looking for Jesus, the individual who had been hailed as king of the Jews, the troublemaker who had caused the commotion in the Temple? Does it not seem more probable, he argues, that the Romans ordered the Jews to arrest Jesus and then bring him to Pilate? This interpretation would tally with John's account that Jesus had been arrested by a cohort of Roman soldiers and held during the night by the Jews without any charges pressed against him.

We can now view the events after the "cleansing of the Temple," with new insight. The situation in Jerusalem was fraught with danger. For almost a week Jesus had been preaching his doctrine of a new kingdom that could be interpreted by the Romans only as sedition. Pilate wanted Jesus apprehended and brought to trial. The chief priests knew that if Jesus persisted in such talk before Pilate, it would mean his execution.*

There was but one way for the Jews to secure an acquittal of Jesus on charges of sedition, says Justice Cohn, and that was for the Jewish leaders to persuade Jesus to plead not guilty to any accusation. And thus it came about that Jesus was detained and an informal, unofficial hearing was held before an undisclosed number of justices, just as the Gospel of John states.

But at this informal hearing Jesus would not cooperate. When the high priest asked, "Are you the Christ, the Son of the Blessed?" he expected a denial. Instead, Jesus answered: "I am; and you will see the Son of man sitting on the right hand of Power . . ."

The high priest knew, says Justice Cohn, that such an assertion by Jesus before Pilate would be equal to a confession of treason and would spell death for Jesus. With his refusal to heed the advice of the high priest to deny all messianic aspirations and all claims to the throne of King David, there was no choice but for the high priest to turn Jesus over to the Romans, says Justice Cohn.

Thus all roads lead to Pontius Pilate.

Though Pilate is a historical figure who for ten years (26–36 A.D.) was procurator of Judea, the evangelists succeeded in turning him into a fictional character. Whereas the Roman historians like Philo saw him as a corrupt, avaricious, murderous governor who had to be removed from his post by Emperor Tiberius for his excessive cruelty, the evangelists portrayed him as a Jesus-loving hu-

---

*This aspect of the trial of Jesus will be analyzed in the next chapter.

manist devoted to justice and mercy. In their hands, Pilate emerged as a weak-minded, dim-witted, well-meaning but cowardly buffoon who, though in command of several legions, was cowed by a small, unarmed Jewish rabble.

With wry amusement scholars note how the evangelists deftly used the trial of Jesus before Pilate to escalate the ill will toward the Jews while giving Pilate successive new coats of whitewash.

Here is how Mark saw the trial in 70 A.D., in Rome: Pilate asks Jesus if he is King of the Jews, and when Jesus answers, "Thou sayest it," Pilate is convinced that he is innocent. Nevertheless, he personally scourges Jesus and hands him to the Roman soldiers to be crucified.

In Matthew, written ten years later in Alexandria, Pilate washes his hands of all guilt and transfers it to the Jews. Although he sentences Jesus to death, he does not personally scourge him, as in Mark, but delegates the task to his soldiers.

In Luke's Gospel, written in Antioch about ten years after Matthew, Pilate has mellowed into a humanist. He does not personally scourge Jesus, nor does he command his soldiers to do so. Luke implies that the Jews did it.

Though John states in his Gospel (written circa 110–140 A.D.) that Pilate personally scourges Jesus and hands him over to the Roman soldiers to be mocked, he now has Pilate declare that Jesus is not guilty after all. Whereas in the three synoptic Gospels it is Pilate who orders the crucifixion, in John's Gospel Pilate tells the Jews to do it themselves.

There is an interesting passage in Matthew's account of the trial that may have echoes in Shakespeare. Matthew informs us that Pilate has a wife in Jerusalem whose name (legend tells us) is Procula. She makes an unexpected appearance at the trial in the courtyard of the Antonia Fortress to implore Pilate not to "find fault" with Jesus but to set him free.★

Is this scene of Procula pleading for the life of Jesus reminiscent of the scene in *The Merchant of Venice* where another woman, Portia, pleads the case of Antonio?★★ Some literary critics think that this play is a symbolic recapitulation of the trial of Jesus—Antonio representing Jesus, Shylock the stand-in for Jehovah, and Portia modeled on Procula.

The famed contract of a pound of flesh to be taken out of an unspecified portion of Antonio's body should he forfeit his bond is based on the law of talion—an eye for an eye, a tooth for a tooth—and a religion for a religion. The pound of flesh Shylock is to get from Antonio represents a symbolic circumcision; thus, if Antonio loses, he would have to become a Jew through that symbolic rite.

But what about the other half of this law of talion? That would demand that should Shylock lose, he would have to become a Christian. This is exactly the option the Duke imposes on Shylock after Portia outwits him. Paradoxically, had Procula won her case and Jesus been set free, there would have been no Christianity.

The whitewashing of Pilate continued to escalate in postcanonical literature at such a fast pace that by the

★Even though her intercession was for naught, the Greek Orthodox Church canonized her. She did not, however, make the Vatican social register of saints.

★★This scene with Portia is especially astounding since women attorneys were unheard of in Shakespeare's day. Also, is it perhaps more than coincidence that Antonio is the name of the protagonist, for Antonia was the name of the tower where Jesus was held prisoner?

fourth century he was headed for sainthood. But he was cheated out of that honor by the Battle of the Milvian Bridge (312 A.D.). Here Emperor Constantine, the victor, saw a cross in the sky, which precipitated his conversion to Christianity. With that conversion and subsequent ascent of the Christians to power in the Empire, there was no further need to softsoap the Romans, and Pilate was deprived of his chance for sainthood.

Though the evangelists went out of their way to portray Pilate as a compassionate, merciful judge, Jesus did not cooperate with him any more than he did with the high priest. In fact, he even taunted Pilate. When Pilate said, "Do you not know that I have the power to release you and power to crucify you?" Jesus defiantly answered, "You can have no power against me, except it might be given you from heaven." Just as the high priest had suspected, Jesus was on a collision course with the Roman Empire. Had Jesus set the stage for the fulfillment of his third prediction that he would be crucified?

Throughout this trial before Pilate, there is but one dominant figure, that of Jesus. Whatever one's faith, one cannot help but admire and respect the courage of this Jew who defied Rome. When Pilate asked him with contempt, "So, you are king?," Jesus boldly answered: "You say I am king. For this reason was I born, and for this I have come into the world, to bear witness to the truth."

The fear of the high priest is confirmed. Pilate sentenced Jesus to death by crucifixion for treason. Jesus walked from Fortress Antonia to Golgotha with his cross upon his back.

We now come to the fifth and last milestone—the crucifixion. We cannot but be touched by the agony of Jesus when he turned his eyes toward heaven and uttered the now famous cry, "My God, my God, why hast Thou forsaken me?"* And we cannot help but be embittered by the mirth of the Romans at his death. The Gospels relate that it was the Jewish multitude that wept at the scene of the crucifixion, not the Romans, who were busy playing dice for his clothes. Neither Pontius Pilate nor the disciples of Jesus showed up to mourn his death at Golgotha. In spite of all the whitewashing of Pilate, the Gospel evidence consistently points to a Roman atrocity, not a miscarriage of Jewish justice.

We have seen how the evangelists consistently fashioned the life of Jesus within the framework of the Old Testament to give legitimacy to his messianic aspirations. Amazingly enough, they also framed his death and rising within this Jewish perception. This view was recently expounded by an Orthodox Jew, Professor Pinchas Lapide, formerly of the Bar-Ilan University in Israel.

Dr. Lapide states that the Jewish tradition includes six accounts of God reawakening the dead, three of them in the Old Testament** and three in the Talmud. He sees no Jewish religious reason why Jesus could not have been the seventh "dead Jew revived by the will of God." He flatly denies, however, that Jesus, risen or not, was either a messiah of Israel or the son of God. But the "reawakening" itself, he says, "was a Jewish affair."

The Church Fathers, too, saw it as a Jewish affair. They point out that in the same way Isaac carried the wood for his sacrificial altar on his shoulders to Mount Moriah, so Jesus carried the cross for his crucifixion on his shoulders to Mount Golgotha. Saint Augustine compares the thicket in which the ram caught his horns to

---

*To his last, Jesus was quoting from the Old Testament. In this case from Psalm 22:1.
**Kings 17:22; II Kings 4:34, and 13:12.

the crown of thorns worn by Jesus. And Saint Ambrose perceptively stated: "Isaac is the prototype for a suffering Christ."

A psychic bond links three famed sacrifices of a child in the name of the "father"—Isaac, Iphigenia, and Jesus —in a fascinating interplay of Jewish, pagan, and Christian themes.

In the Genesis story, Abraham stands to gain nothing by sacrificing his son Isaac. God promises him no favors. Faith carries him to Mount Moriah; hope sustains him. The sacrifice is never consummated; an angel stays his hand, and a sacrificial lamb is substituted for Isaac.

The *Iliad* story is the reverse. An oracle advises Agamemnon, the commander of the Greek forces, that only by sacrificing his daughter Iphigenia as an atonement for a trifling crime he has committed will the gods give him the favorable winds he needs to set sail for Troy. Without further ado, Agamemnon cuts the throat of his daughter.

In the Gospel story, Jesus, like Abraham, has nothing to gain personally. In the Jewish scenario, the final sacrifice is the ram; in the Christian, Jesus himself is the sacrificial lamb. In the Jewish scenario Isaac lives; in the Christian, Jesus dies.

Some Jewish theologians feel that the sacrifice of Isaac has greater spiritual kinship to that of Jesus than most Jews are willing to concede. Several Talmudic commentators hold that Isaac himself, not the ram, was actually sacrificed by Abraham, and that through that sacrifice Israel was redeemed. Chapter 22 in Genesis, they point out, states that both Abraham and Isaac went to Mount Moriah. But Genesis does not state that both returned. It explicitly states that only Abraham returned, and the sages ask, "Where was Isaac?"

Just as the evangelists quote disconnected sentences

from the Old Testament to prove that the messiahship of Jesus was in fulfillment of prophecy, so these Talmudic sages deduce from disconnected sentences in the Old Testament that Isaac was actually sacrificed by Abraham and revived by God. A famed Talmudist states it this way: "When Abraham bound his son Isaac on the altar, and slew him, and burned him, the lad was reduced to ashes. . . . And the Holy One, blessed be He, brought down the life-giving dew and revived him, whereupon the ministering angels proceeded to say the resurrection benediction, 'Blessed is He who revives the dead.' "*

Other Jewish sages add that Isaac offered himself willingly as a sacrifice (though they made no allusion to Jesus). And how do they deduce this? The theory is that Isaac was thirty-seven years old at the time and the aged Abraham would not have been able to bind him had Isaac not cooperated.

It could be argued that the Jews as well as the Christians have a "trinity"—the former centered around the *akedah* (as the sacrifice of Isaac is called in Jewish liturgy), and the latter centered around the cross. In the Jewish "trinity," the commander, the executioner, and the victim are three separate individuals—God who commands Abraham to sacrifice Isaac, Abraham who carries out God's will, and Isaac who is the sacrifice.

In the Christian trinity the commander, executioner, and victim are all combined in one individual, in Jesus, who informs God he will sacrifice himself.

---

*The interested reader is referred to a most evocative book, *The Last Trial: On the Legends and Lore of the Command to Abraham to Offer Isaac as a Sacrifice* by Shalom Spiegel (The Jewish Publication Society, Philadelphia, 1967). It gives all the innumerable Talmudic and rabbinic references to this aspect of the sacrifice of Isaac.

Thus it could be said that with the *akedah*, Isaac is the passive victim through whom Israel is redeemed. With the cross, Jesus is the active victim through whom mankind is to be saved. Each, in its own way, fulfills an unconscious wish that encapsulates its own *Weltanschauung*—world view.

Did Jesus, as he lingered on the cross waiting for death, think he had founded a new religion, a new church, a new hierarchy? Says Charles Guignebert, "It never crossed his mind." Jesus was born a Jew, lived the life of a Jew, and died as a Jew with a Jewish prayer on his lips. He was made a Christian posthumously.

We have now taken two walks with Jesus, one down the Christian theological road, the other along the Jewish historical road. But if faith answers all questions, the scholar's inquiry leaves nagging questions in its wake. Even granting that all the historical evidence presented is true, the main enigma remains unanswered. Scholars ask: Why was Jesus tried for treason by the Romans? Certainly, being proclaimed a symbolic son of David by a small, messiah-intoxicated crowd at one of the gates of Jerusalem did not constitute a rebellion in the eyes of the Romans. What is the real meaning of the "cleansing of the Temple"? Is it a euphemistic phrase that hides an unacceptable truth? Why are the synoptic evangelists so intent on showing that Jesus was sentenced to death by the Jews at a trial by the Sanhedrin if there was no such trial or sentence according to John? Why are all four evangelists so intent on shifting the blame for the death of Jesus from the Romans to the Jews? Why do they insist on the historically untenable explanation that the Jews had to get permission from the Romans to carry out a death sentence? Are they trying to hide some unpalatable facts? If so, what are they reluctant to reveal?

To many of the devout, accustomed to thinking of Jesus as a prince of peace, it is difficult if not downright abhorrent to conceive of him as a man of war who tried to seize power in an open rebellion against Rome. What is more, to propagate such a notion in the days of the evangelists, when the Romans were throwing Christians to the lions, would have been downright dangerous.

Nevertheless, the melancholy task of the historian is to set faith aside, ignore expedience, and view facts dispassionately. In our search for answers, let us now join a new safari of scholars who will unveil a third face of Jesus—Jesus as a messiah armed.

Chapter 5

The Political Road to the Cross

In the year 30 A.D., on the fifteenth day of Nisan according to the Jewish calendar, Jerusalem was crowded with pilgrims who had come from every part of Palestine to celebrate Passover. Excitement ran high. A rebellion in the provinces had just been quelled with blood and crucifixions by Pontius Pilate.

Rumors of another revolt were rife. People were talking about a new Jewish messiah named Jesus, who had entered Jerusalem on the colt of an ass in the manner that the prophets had predicted the messiah would arrive. To the Romans, who had crucified dozens of such messiah-rebels in the past, this talk spelled trouble. Pontius Pilate also feared a new wave of unrest. He left his mistress in Caesaria, his administrative capital north of Jerusalem, and came to the city to take personal charge, bringing an extra cohort of legionnaires with him, ringing Jerusalem with steel.

This is the scene when the curtain goes up on our third view of Jesus as a rebel, leading an unsuccessful rebellion against Rome. Jesus, some scholars contend, was not only thought of as a religious savior by his adherents, but was also looked upon as their leader in a revolt against Rome.*

Palestine in the days of Jesus was occupied by Rome in the same way Hungary, Poland, and Czechoslovakia were occupied by Russia after World War II. One revolt after another swept Judea after the death of King Herod in 4 B.C., as patriots and messiahs stirred the population into successive revolts. The center of rebel activity was Galilee. Here, around 6 A.D., arose a new party named the Zealots, which had received its name from Phineas, the nephew of Moses. Phineas officially was named the first "zealot" (i.e., zealous one) in Jewish history for slaying Cozbi, the daughter of a Midianite priest, when he found her fornicating with a Jew. This incident, enshrined in the Old Testament,** has embarrassed Jewish theologians because Moses himself was married to the daughter of a Midianite priest. To the credit of the Old Testament authors, they never allowed an embarrassment to stand between them and the truth.

---

*Readers interested in a presentation of Jesus as a pre-Marxist proletarian revolutionary are referred to the dreary volume by Karl Kautzky, entitled *Foundations of Christianity* (S. A. Russell, New York, 1953). It is the usual Marxist cant—the Jews and the Romans were an exploiting capitalist class and Jesus the hero of the working class out to establish a communist dictatorship of the proletariat. No matter what country or century, books by Communists always read like the same page from *Pravda*.

**Numbers 25:6–16.

The founder of the Zealot party was Judah the Galileean, a countryman of Jesus and the childhood hero of
Galileean children. The motto of the Zealots, "If any man
would come after me, let him deny himself and take up
his cross and follow me," was later popularized by Jesus.★
As the fate of a Zealot if caught by the Romans was
crucifixion, it was only natural that they became an un-
derground party in Palestine.

The most notorious among the Zealots was a gang
known as the Sicarii, mostly Galileeans. They were a
secret band of super patriots whose specialty was killing
Roman occupation officials with daggers known as *sicarii*,
hence the name. The Romans, on the other hand, viewed
them as "death squads." It was these Galileean Zealots
and Sicarii daggermen who had bedeviled the Romans
for three decades with one bloody revolt after another.
And now, in the year 30 A.D., trouble for Pontius Pilate
hung in the Passover air—the threat of yet another rebellion, this time led by a Jew named Jesus.

Who was this Jesus who had entered Jerusalem most
humbly, on the colt of an ass, and was welcomed by the
population with cries of "Hosanna, son of David"? Was
he a harmless crackpot? A misguided messiah? Or was
he perhaps the leader of a new Zealot uprising? These
self-proclaimed saviors, whether crackpots or messiahs,
the Romans knew, could inflame the people with words
quicker than a torch could set fire to paper. Jerusalem
was a tinderbox. Any small incident might incite the Jews
to another rebellion. Pilate's decision was to watch what
this Jew Jesus would do next before taking action.

The evangelists are strangely silent about these tur-
bulent times, when Jews and Romans were locked in an

★See S. G. F. Brandon, *Jesus and the Zealots*. Scribner & Sons,
London, 1967. Also Mark 8:34.

embrace of mutual hatred and contempt. They move Jesus across the bloodstained year 30 A.D., as in a dreamland of peace and contentment. Yet, to ensure some historical credibility, they do leave spoors of strife behind them like geological strata. Each evangelist preserved fragments of a Judean–Roman conflict, vaguely depicting Jesus as leading a band of "disciples" without a specific goal. These fragments are strewn throughout the four narratives, and not until scholars isolated and rearranged them into a sequence did they reveal an actual conflict.

Is there any evidence in the Gospels that Jesus might be such a warrior-messiah bent on wresting the throne of King David from the Romans? There is, aver many scholars.★ Such evidence, they claim, can be clearly seen in the Gospels if we leave out theology and stick to the main story outline. If we do that, then six events in the Gospel narratives will reveal with dramatic intensity a portrait of Jesus as a rebel against Rome.

The six events these scholars ask us to concentrate on are: The mission of the twelve apostles; the triumphant entry of Jesus into Jerusalem; the hidden meaning of the "cleansing of the Temple"; the peculiar circumstances surrounding the arrest of Jesus; the riddle of Barabbas; and the last, the triple crucifixion at Golgotha. Each is a puzzle that must be solved to yield the clues to Jesus as a rebel and to the meaning of his predictions.

The first puzzle is the function of the twelve apostles. It is hard to fathom their mission. What are they supposed to do? They are seemingly an inept and cowardly lot on whom Jesus cannot depend and whom he constantly has

---

★Two most exciting recent books on this aspect of Jesus as a Zealot are *On the Trial of Jesus* by Paul Winter (Walter de Gruyter, Berlin, 1961) and *Jesus and the Zealots* by S. G. F. Brandon.

to rebuke. They fail in the mission of proselytizing, and at the first sign of danger they desert Jesus. Peter, in fact, denies his master three times even before there is any apparent danger. They are not present at the crucifixion, nor are they the ones to bury Jesus. And they are the last to whom Jesus presents himself after his resurrection.

Could it be, reflects Protestant theologian Johannes Lehmann,★ that the job of the apostles is not that of religious missionaries but of messianic warriors enlisted in the Zealot cause?

If we view the twelve apostles as Zealots fighting in the cause of freedom, we suddenly understand why they scattered at the first sign of trouble. If caught by the Romans as rebels, they would have been promptly crucified, the Roman cure for insurrection. Viewed thus, the advice of Jesus to his disciples makes sense. He gave them strict instructions to contact only Israelites. They were to stay in one place only long enough to deliver the message, then take off. If they felt they were under suspicion, they were to disappear quickly from the scene. They were to exercise great caution in speech and action. "Behold," Jesus told his disciples, "I send you forth as sheep in the midst of wolves; be ye therefore as wise as serpents, and harmless as doves." In other words, act like undercover agents.

Luke best preserves a picture of Jesus as a revolutionary. On the eve of the coming insurrection, his small band of disciples start a quarrel over what office each will hold after victory. Jesus points out that dedicated revolutionaries do not seek personal advantage. Nevertheless, he promises that they will sit on thrones as judges in the new state. Then Jesus says "Let him who has no sword

★ *Rabbi J.* by Johannes Lehmann (New York: Stein & Day, 1970).

sell his mantle . . . because in Scripture it is written 'And he was counted among the outlaws.' These words in Scripture, I tell you, must find fulfillment in me."*

Some theologians have suggested that the disciples had to exercise caution because of the hostility of scribes, Sadducees, and Pharisees. But this does not make sense, since Jesus preached his kingdom of God throughout Galilee and Judea for an entire year without getting into trouble with any of them. The trouble started, as we have seen, only after he entered Jerusalem and became a political suspect in the eyes of the Romans.

Scholars like Oscar Cullman, Paul Winter, John Brandon, Johannes Lehmann, and Joel Carmichael point out that there are numerous indications in the Gospels themselves that several of the apostles were Zealots.

First, there is Simon, openly so acknowledged by Luke, who calls him "Simon, the Zealot." Mark tries to hide this fact by calling him "Simon the Canaean," which is Aramaic for "Zealot."

Then there is Judas Iskariot, whose name is usually explained to mean "Judas, the man from Keriot." But, scholars point out, there is no such town. The name, they say, means "Judas, the Sicarii"—that is, Judas the Daggerman. The Hebrew and Aramaic alphabets consist only of consonants. Thus the words *sicarii* and *iscariot* are both rendered in Hebrew by the same consonants "skr."**

Simon Peter† was also known as Simon bar Jona, usually explained to mean "Simon, the son of Jona," since

---

*Luke 22:37–38.
**Incidentally, Paul himself was once mistaken for such a daggerman (Acts 21:28) by a Roman captain, who said "Are you not the Egyptian . . . who recently stirred up a revolt and led thousands of daggermen into the wilderness?"
†Also known simply as Peter.

bar means "son." But "bar Jona" can also spell *baryon* (plural *baryonim*), meaning "open country" in Aramaic. Because the Zealots fled to the hills in the "open country" of Galilee when pursued by the Romans, they were also known as *baryonim*. Simon Peter, who was a Galileean by birth, was thus called Simon baryon—in other words, Simon the "open country" Zealot.

Another name given the Zealots was "men of thunder," describing their warlike natures. Interestingly enough, the apostles James, the elder, and his brother John are called *boanerges*, the Aramaic word for "thunder."

Martyrdom awaited any Zealot if caught. Such a fate did indeed befall eight of the twelve apostles who eventually were captured, mostly by the Romans. Simon Peter was crucified head-down in Rome, and Andrew was crucified on an X-shaped cross (known today as a St. Andrew's cross). James the younger was crucified in Egypt, and Jude was tortured to death in Persia. Bartholomew was flayed to death, and Thomas was martyred in a most unusual way—by a shower of arrows while he was at prayer. Matthew died a martyr in Ethiopia, and Simon was crucified in the traditional manner. Thus we see it was not the Jews who killed the apostles because they were Christians, but the Romans who executed them because they were suspected of being Zealots.

The remaining four disciples met with varied ends unconnected with the Romans. James the elder was beheaded by orders of King Herod Agrippa, the only one to die a violent death not at the behest of the Romans. Judas, according to the evangelists, committed suicide. The only ones to die of natural causes were Philip and John.

We can understand why the Gospels would make

every attempt to tone down the facts of the real nature of the apostles. Everything that might appear dangerous from a political view had to be filtered out and symbolized. Thus, for instance, a quest for a new kingdom of David became "a kingdom of God," in the Gospels. After the first century A.D., some seventy years after the death of Jesus, Christianity was no longer a Jewish creed but a new religion; the vast majority of Christians were no longer Jews but converted pagans. To them, a symbolic representation of Jesus as a harmless, persecuted messiah was more acceptable than the harsh reality of him as a feared Jewish rebel.

But it was not easy to filter out all conspiratorial elements. There was still the memory of survivors. Thus, though each evangelist suppressed what he thought was dangerous to the new movement, he nevertheless had to weave in enough historical material to lend credence to his Gospel. But the further each Gospel writer was in time from the date of the crucifixion, the more license he could take with history. Thus, Mark, the closest to that date, has the most historical foundation, and John, who was the farthest away, has the least.

To quote Lehmann, again: "The evangelists are interpreters not biographers. . . . They did not write history; they invented it." Yet each of the synoptic Gospel writers retained sayings of Jesus that present him, not only as a prince of peace but also as a harbinger of war. His followers believed he was a war messiah come to restore the Kingdom of Israel, not in heaven but on earth.

But the Zealot membership of the apostles is only the first indicator in a series of six that lead some scholars to the view that Jesus was in search of an earthly throne in addition to a heavenly one. Let us now rejoin Jesus and his band as they reached Jericho on their march to Jerusalem. Here, an electrifying political episode took place. For the first time Jesus was openly proclaimed "son of David." A blind beggar sitting by the roadside, hearing it was Jesus passing by, held out his hands to solicit alms, crying out, "Pity me, son of David."

Such language spelled danger. If a Roman soldier or a collaborator were to hear it, all of them could be crucified as conspirators. Several onlookers did try to stop the beggar, but heedlessly he shouted even more loudly: "Pity me, son of David." And, Jesus, who up to then had forbidden anyone to call him "messiah" or "son of God" or "son of David," did not do so on this occasion.

Is this beggar symbolic of the Jewish people kept in thralldom by the Romans, and is Jesus depicted here as the messiah-king on his way to restore the crown of David to the throne of Judah? Let us review the events that followed.

Jesus and his troupe of Zealot-apostles arrived at Bethphage only six miles from Jerusalem. Here Jesus stopped and ordered one of his disciples to go to a nearby village, where, he said, a foal would be tethered that had never been ridden by anyone. His instructions were to bring the foal to him. Should anyone question the disciple, the secret password was to be, "The master needs him."

This implies conspiracy, a plan replete with secret codes. But why a foal? Jesus himself supplied the answer to his wondering disciples. In order to fulfill prophecy, says Jesus, for was it not written in Zechariah, "Rejoice greatly, O daughter of Zion; behold the king cometh unto thee, riding upon an ass, even unto a colt, the foal of an ass."

The people of Jerusalem knew their Bible, knew what Zechariah had said. The word that the son of David was coming flew along the road from Jericho to Jerusalem on the wings of hope and gossip. As Jesus and his entourage, now grown into a "multitude," neared Jerusalem, the people went wild. They spread their cloaks on the ground for him to ride on. And all along the road the people shouted, "Hosanna on high." . . . "Blessed is he who comes in the name of the Lord, even the King of Israel."

As Jesus entered Jerusalem, according to tradition through the Golden Gate, the shouts of "hosanna" grew in intensity. He was an unmitigated success. The Pharisees, scribes, and elders were worried, however, and admonished Jesus to restrain the crowd. But Jesus replied, "I tell you, if they are silent the stones will cry out." In other words, nothing now could stop him.

Most people think the word "hosanna" is some kind of benign greeting like "Hail, hail" or "peace be unto you." Such is not the case. The word "hosanna" in both Hebrew and Aramaic means "save us." What the people along the road to Jerusalem and at its gates were shouting was, "Save us, free us, Jesus, son of David"; in other words, deliver us from the Romans. Nothing theological here. The people cried out, not for the kingdom of heaven, but for a kingdom of David then and there on earth.

John adds an important detail. He says the "great multitude took palm branches from the palm trees and went forth to meet him." This is of great significance because in those days a palm branch was not a symbol of peace but one of triumph, presented as an honor to the victor, to the conqueror. Thus, throwing palm branches under the feet of Jesus signified a victory celebration over the Roman oppressors and homage to the conqueror, Jesus.

These cries of "hosanna" were words of sedition, an

invitation to disaster. Can anyone imagine a crowd in Amsterdam or Paris, during the Nazi-occupation days, marching down a main thoroughfare, shouting, "Save us from the Nazis, son of Liberty." The Gestapo would have had that "liberator" in their torture basements in no time. No wonder Pharisees, scribes, and priests were worried. But where were the Romans? The Gospels do not say. Perhaps Pilate thought it best to keep a low profile so as not to further inflame the excited crowds thronging into Jerusalem to celebrate Passover. The last thing he wanted at this time was to send another report to his emperor about yet another failure to keep order.

The next day, however, Pilate did march on Jerusalem. There had been another provocation, some kind of melee at the Temple, again by that "troublemaker" Jesus about whom he had already had several alarming reports. Euphemistically, the Gospels have labeled that incident the "cleansing of the Temple." This is the third crisis point.

Was the incident in the Temple little more than a minor brouhaha in an Eastern bazaar, or was it a military action? From the way the synoptic evangelists describe it, the "cleansing of the Temple" was just a caper—Jesus singlehandedly overturning the tables of the money-changers and starting a little stampede of sellers, buyers, sheep, and oxen. Yet nobody was angry at him, not even the moneychangers who seemingly just listened indifferently to Jesus accusing them of having turned the Temple into a "den of robbers."

John, however, adds that Jesus made a whip of chords with which to drive the moneychangers out of the Temple. Here we have a different picture of Jesus, no longer a prince of peace. Here we see violence at work, with Jesus in the midst of it. But does it stand to reason that only one man armed with a mere whip could cow hundreds of vendors and moneychangers into instant surrender?

Let us transpose this so-called "cleansing of the Temple" into modern times for a more balanced perspective. What would happen if a bearded gentleman were to arrive on Monday of Holy Week in a Fiat at Piazza San Pietro (Vatican Square) in Rome and start beating the vendors of crucifixes, rosaries, and candles on the steps of St. Peter's, saying he was a messiah come to cleanse the churches? Would no one pay any attention to him? Or would he be arrested as a disturber of the peace? Or would he be given a psychiatric examination and thrown into a mental ward? One thing is certain—most of the vendors of religious bric-a-brac in the stalls around St. Peter's would not take flight. They would probably give him a beating before the police arrived.

The fracas at the Temple as described in the Gospels is implausible. What makes it even impossible is that the Temple was not a small synagogue on a postage-stamp–size lot. It was more like a medieval walled city, a magnificent, fortresslike structure, 600 feet wide and 1350 feet long, surrounded by a stone wall, with four towers and two fortified entrances. The Temple was the crowning work of King Herod and had taken fifty years to complete.

The original Temple built by King Solomon (circa 973–933 B.C.) had been destroyed by the Babylonians in 586 B.C. but was rebuilt by 515 B.C. after the Jewish return from the Babylonian exile. This Temple must have been a sorry-looking affair, architecturally no more imposing than a small-town Moolah temple, for even the Prophet Haggai complained it was a depressing sight. It was, therefore, ironic that the Idumean King Herod, one of the most hated men in Jewish history, should have been the architect of the new Temple, one of the wonders of the world, which impressed not only the effete Romans but also became revered by the Orthodox Jews.*

The Temple was not just a house of worship. The sanctuary was but a small segment of the total Temple, which consisted of a huge complex of buildings, with housing for attendants and priests, storehouses, and a number of courtyards for all sorts of activities. It was served and protected by a gigantic staff of some twenty thousand functionaries—police, priests, office workers, attendants, bankers, and vendors of pigeons, sheep, and oxen (instead of vendors of crucifixes, rosaries, and candles as in Italian cathedrals today).

The Temple courtyard was an imposing sight. Along most of its east wall ran a colonnade of 162 pillars of white marble known as Solomon's Portico. The average Gospel reader thinks there was moneychanging inside the sanctuary, but such was not the case. It took place in this colonnade, which also served as a public marketplace. Here the merchants congregated. The Temple grounds, but not the sanctuary, also housed an international bank that, like the Vatican today, handled vast sums of money to service its complex network of business activities. And, like the Vatican today, the Temple, too, was protected by a special police force, as well as by the nearby Roman army.

When Jesus entered Jerusalem, there was a permanent force of some six hundred Roman legionnaires in the Fortress Antonia, the main fort at the Temple wall.

Now, imagine thousands of pilgrims from all over Judea arrived to celebrate the Passover holiday in Jeru-

---

*Today Orthodox Jews still kiss the stones in the Western Wall of the Temple built by the hated Herod.

salem, there to buy their sacrificial doves, sheep, and oxen, which were as central to the Jewish sacrifice cult two thousand years ago as the Mass is to Catholic worship today. Imagine Jerusalem police patrolling the area, Roman soldiers around the corner to keep things under control, hundreds of vendors and moneychangers buying, selling, preparing for Passover. And here comes Jesus. Singlehandedly he beats up the moneychangers and vendors, overturns the money tables, and starts a stampede by liberating the sheep and oxen through crowds of pilgrims.

According to the Gospels, nobody did anything—not the police, not the vendors who saw their merchandise disappear, not the moneylenders who saw their profits spilled into the gutter, not the Roman soldiers who must have viewed the turmoil with some apprehension. The Gospel accounts of Jesus' "cleansing of the Temple" are hard to believe, say scholars. It could not have happened this way then, any more than it could happen in the Vatican today.

Now imagine further that after this turmoil, Jesus calmly gathered listeners around him, preaching and teaching for the rest of the week, until Friday, when he was finally arrested.

Nevertheless, improbable or not, all four evangelists say Jesus did enter Jerusalem, did go to the Temple, did overturn the tables of the moneychangers, and did come back, day after day, to Jerusalem, to the Temple, there to preach openly in full freedom, with the police and soldiers doing nothing.

How can we explain these improbable events? Scholars who hold to the view that Jesus was a rebel against Rome have developed a theory that would clarify these contradictions by viewing the "Temple cleansing" not as a caper but as an insurrection. Their view is that Jesus and his disciples, and the "multitude" that joined him along the road from Jericho, were mostly armed Zealots, that they seized the Temple by force and held it for five days, after which the rebellion collapsed. Jesus was later arrested by the Jews, they say, and held in protective custody by them. But the Romans, learning of this subterfuge, demanded that Jesus be handed over to them. Viewed this way, the unfolding of the events of the arrest of Jesus by the Jews, the trial by Pilate, and the execution for sedition by the Romans has a logic and sequence that make historic sense.

But is there any evidence in the Gospels for such a supposition? Yes, say these scholars. Though the evangelists tried to screen out all seditious elements in the life of Jesus by presenting the seizure of the Temple as a "theological cleansing," they could not exclude all incriminating evidence of force because there probably were too many oral histories circulating among Christian converts that referred to an actual Temple takeover. We can find such confirmation in Gospels and other sources— puzzling references, isolated sentences that make no sense unless one views them as remnants describing a siege of the Temple.

Roman historians like Tacitus seem to take it for granted that Jesus was an armed Zealot who was executed by Pontius Pilate (he mentions no arrest by the Jews). The Roman governor of Bythinia and prefect of Egypt stated (as quoted by Lactantius, one of the early Church Fathers) that Jesus was a leader of a band of robbers (a euphemism for Zealots) numbering over nine hundred men. A medieval copy of Josephus in Hebrew states that

Jesus had more than two thousand armed men at the Mount of Olives.★

Luke states that eighteen people were killed by the fall of the Tower of Siloam, one of the towers in the walls surrounding the Temple.★★ The tower could not just fall by itself. If Jesus did indeed take the Temple by force, then the Romans could have stormed the Tower of Siloam, destroying it in that action. Luke also speaks of the Galileeans having their blood spilled with that of Pilate,† indicating a clash of arms between the forces of Jesus and Pilate.

What do we have thus far in the theory that Jesus was a Zealot conspirator? We may suppose that six or maybe all of the apostles were either Zealots or Zealot sympathizers; that eight of the twelve apostles caught by the Romans were crucified or tortured to death, not for the crime of being Christians but for that of being suspected Zealots; that Jesus constantly admonished his followers to arm themselves, to sell their mantles to buy swords, to set brother against brother;‡ that there was fighting at the tower of Siloam after the seizure of the Temple, and

---

★This statement is not found in any other version. There are two explanations—that this Hebrew version is a fraud, or that the Church was successful in expunging this reference in all other editions.

★★Luke 13:4.

†Luke 13:1.

‡Or, as the Gospels so forthrightly state: "And brother shall deliver brother to death, and the father, the child, and the children shall rise up against parents, and cause them to be put to death." (Matthew 10:21) "But these mine enemies which would not that I reign over them, bring them hither, and slay them before me." (Luke 19:27) "Think not that I am come to bring peace to earth. I come not to bring peace, but a sword." (Matthew 10:34)

that there was bloodshed between the Galileeans and Romans.

Interesting but not convincing, a modern-day doubting Thomas might rebut. And he would be right. These assorted facts, however, must be viewed within the context of events yet to come. This brings us to the fourth main event in our search for clues pointing to Jesus and his apostles as rebels, namely, the curious circumstances surrounding the Last Supper. In this cluster of circumstances we have four clues, each hinting at Jesus as a leader of a Zealot uprising.

The first clue is the conspiratorial air surrounding the arrangements for the Last Supper. Before entering Jerusalem Jesus talked like a secret agent. He sent two of his disciples to the city with instructions to contact a man carrying a pot of water and give him the secret password, and he in turn would show the disciples the secret place where the Passover meal would be served. Why this secrecy? There was no arrest order out for Jesus. Every day he appeared in the Temple preaching there openly. Whom was he afraid of? The Jews or the Romans?

The arrest of Jesus is the second clue. John states* that Pilate sent a cohort of soldiers to arrest Jesus. A Roman cohort was composed of four hundred to six hundred men. Why would such a force be necessary to arrest an unarmed Jesus with no more than twelve disciples in his company? In all four Gospels, we find subtle hints of an armed struggle. In fact, Jesus told Simon Peter who had drawn his sword: "Put your sword back into its place; for those who take to the sword will perish by the sword."

This leads to the third clue. It is at this point that

---

*John 18:3.

the twelve disciples turned tail and fled. Why? Did they realize they were outnumbered and if captured by the Romans they would be faced with crucifixion for sedition?

Maybe it was at this point, some scholars surmise, that the disciples realized that Jesus was more interested in becoming a messiah than he was in restoring the throne of King David, that he really meant literally what he had preached at Caesaria Philippi. Could it be that at the point where Jesus forbade them to fight, they gave up on him as their military leader and fled?

The fourth clue is contained in the statement made in John's Gospel that Jesus was brought by the Roman soldiers to the house of Annas, the brother-in-law of the high priest—where he questioned Jesus about his disciples. The *Oxford Annotated Bible* makes the fascinating observation that Annas held an informal trial of Jesus designed to indict him "for training disciples secretly as revolutionaries."* As we see, the roadmarks are consistent. They all point to a "Zealot connection."

We now come to Barabbas—the fifth milestone in our journey of detection—one of the most vexing narratives in the Gospels.

The Barabbas story has the merit of instant believability, if one does not question it. To appease the Jews who clamored for the life of Jesus, say the evangelists, Pilate offered them a deal. They could choose to set free either Jesus or someone named Barabbas, according to a custom known as *privilegium Paschale,* the "privilege of Passover." This Passover custom, according to the evangelists, permitted the procurator of Judea to set free any prisoner the Jews chose. Whom did the Jews want freed?

---

*Pg. 1, 311, footnote.

asks Pilate. According to the Gospels, the crowd wanted Barabbas freed and Jesus condemned.

This is the easy part. Now comes the difficult bit. There has never been such a custom as *privilegium Paschale* among either Jews or Romans. This concept of setting a condemned man free on Passover is found only in the Gospels.

But who is this enigmatic Barabbas? Interestingly enough, the evangelists tell us that he was a Zealot, arrested in a recent insurrection in Jerusalem. What insurrection? There was only a "cleansing of the Temple." Could it be, surmise scholars, that perhaps Barabbas was one of those captured at the battle of the Tower of Siloam, as mentioned in Luke? Could this not be another confirmation of conflict on the Temple grounds?

From a Roman standpoint, the Barabbas episode is incredible. Barabbas was a rebel, caught in an insurrection. And yet, here we see the imperial representative of Emperor Tiberius, supported by an overwhelming military force, cowed by a small, unarmed crowd of Jews, offering to trade a known rebel, Barabbas, for Jesus. Any Roman governor setting a traitor against Rome free in exchange for an avowed friend of Rome, as Jesus was depicted, would have had his head examined—after it was severed from his body. From a theological standpoint, however, it was dramatic and effective. It showed the Romans that the Jews were responsible for the death of Jesus and that the merciful Pilate was frustrated by the ignoble Jews in his noble effort to free Jesus. But history refused to cooperate with this view.

The survival of several noncanonized gospel codices (like the Sinaitic, Syriac, and Armenian)★ has brought to

---

★Abstracted from Paul Winter's study *On the Trial of Jesus*, pg. 95.

light that Barabbas's first name was Jesus. Jesus Christ and Jesus Barabbas! The name "Barabbas" is a contraction for *bar abba*, meaning "the son of the father," in the same way that the name "Johnson" means "the son of John." Thus, the literal translation of Jesus Barabbas is "Jesus, the son of the father" which is precisely what Jesus had been saying all the time that he was.

The fact that the first name of Barabbas was also Jesus gave theological headaches to some Church Fathers, especially to Origen. With his accustomed aplomb in such matters, he wrote that since Barabbas could not have such a holy name as "Jesus," it must have been added by heretics.

This clue that the first name of Barabbas was Jesus has led scholars to speculate on two theories. The first holds that there were two men named Jesus, both of whom had been arrested. One was Jesus of Nazareth, the son of Joseph; the other was Jesus Barabbas, the son of Abba. One of them was wanted for participating in the insurrection in the city. When Pilate learned that Jesus bar Abba was not the man he was looking for, he released Jesus bar Abba and sentenced the second Jesus, Jesus the son of Joseph, to death. Could it be, surmise scholars, that the evangelists shifted the rebellion from Jesus to Barabbas, thus reversing the roles?

The second theory holds that Jesus of Nazareth and Jesus Barabbas were one and the same person; that legend split him into two personalities—one a peaceful messiah, the other a warrior-Zealot. Some scholars believe that the evangelists fashioned that legend into the Barabbas episode.

In the legends of the Greek Orthodox Church, both Jesus and Barabbas were imprisoned in adjacent cells in the Roman Tower of Antonia. Next to the former Tower of Antonia, in Jerusalem today, is a Greek monastery, formerly part of the Antonia Tower grounds. Here is a cell marked "Prison of Christ," and it is here, Greek tradition has it, that both Jesus and Barabbas were imprisoned. Jesus, according to this legend, was the prisoner not of the Jews but of the Romans. If so, it is quite possible that the wrong Jesus was brought to Pilate. Some Gospel codices actually state that the option proposed by Pilate to the Jews was "whom will you that I release to you, Jesus Barabbas or Jesus who is called the Christ?"*

And thus, perhaps, it came about that the evangelists, seeking to explain away the Roman execution of Jesus, presented him as a victim of Jewish leaders instead of as the victim of Roman rapacity. In the pursuit of this apologetic theme, all references to Zealots and uprisings were subtly suppressed. And thus, perhaps, it came about that Barabbas, who had been involved in a bloody insurrection against Rome, was pitted against a "peaceable" Jesus.

But still we have seen no "smoking gun" to prove indisputably that Jesus was a Zealot. Ironically, it is the evangelists themselves who supply that "gun"—the most convincing piece of evidence that he was considered a rebel by Rome. All four Gospel writers agree that the crime of Jesus was spelled out on his death tag by Pilate—*King of the Jews*.

And now we reach our sixth milestone, at the foot of Golgotha. Here also we find verification that Jesus might have started out as a rebel against Rome before becoming the messiah. That evidence was to the right and left of Jesus at Golgotha. Jesus was not the only Jew to be crucified that day. There were three—Jesus and two

---

*See *Catholic Biblical Encyclopedia*, under the heading "Barabbas."

83

other, unnamed Jews crucified to the right and left of him. Who were they, and why were they crucified?

Gospel translations usually state that Jesus was crucified between two thieves. But the Romans did not crucify thieves. The original Greek text says not "thieves" but "rebels." It could well be that the Romans had caught three Zealots (one being Jesus) and executed all three for the same crime in the same manner at the same time. Could it be that perhaps the name of one of the rebels hanging to the right or left of Jesus of Nazareth was Jesus Barabbas ("the man who had been thrown in prison for an insurrection in the city," to quote Luke)?

We can now permit the curtain to descend on this scene of agony—the death of Jesus as a perceived or as an actual Zealot, the unsuccessful aspirant for the crown of King David.

This scenario of Jesus as a rebel also illuminates two contradictory perceptions of the messiah. The Jews thought of their promised messiah as a man of war, sword in hand, shield on arm, entering Jerusalem on a fiery steed. Imagine their surprise when what arrived was a humble carpenter on the colt of an ass, who was ignominiously crucified like a seditious slave. The Jews rejected this parvenu messiah, whereas the downtrodden masses in the Roman Empire accepted him. After two thousand years, the Jews still await their messiah, though the conquering David Ben-Gurion has arrived, reconstituted the State of Israel right under the nosecones of atomic bombs, and departed.

But after almost two thousand years, the Christians, too, are still awaiting the second coming of Jesus as promised in the Gospel of John. When he does come a second time (the Second Advent), will it again be in the image of the old Christian perception of the messiah as a humble artisan on the colt of an ass, or will it this time be in the Jewish perception—the messiah arriving as a conquering hero on a fiery steed?

Repressed ideas have a habit of finding permissible expression in literature through symbol and allegory. Sixty-five years after the death of Jesus, the Jewish concept of the messiah was resurrected in a piece of Christian literature named *The Book of Revelation*, written in 95 A.D. It so strongly mirrored a longing in the Christian soul that, a century later, *Revelation* was made a part of the *New Testament*.

Just as the Jewish messiah was thought of as arriving to smite the oppressors of the Jews, so the Jesus in *Revelation* appears to smite the Roman oppressors of the Christians. And this Jesus in *Revelation* acts no longer like a humble carpenter but as a proud Jewish scion of the House of David. In *Revelation*, Jesus is referred to not by his own name, but as "King of kings," or as "Lord of lords." This is what the *Book of Revelation* says of the new Jesus:

> Then I saw heaven opened, and behold, a white horse. He who sat upon it is . . . clad in a robe dipped in blood. On his robe and his thigh, he has a name inscribed, King of kings, and Lord of lords. . . . From his mouth issued a short sword with which to smite the nations, and he will rule them with a rod of iron.

Though the theory of Jesus as a rebel does clarify many otherwise enigmatic passages in the Gospels, it does not explain countless other clusters of enigmatic sentences. The rebel theory does not explain, for instance, why it was so important to Jesus that he be arrested by the Jews and betrayed by one of his most trusted apostles, why he had to die by crucifixion, and why it had to take place in Jerusalem. These, as we have seen, are all the conditions Jesus himself constantly insisted upon and predicted would happen. Why did Jesus not defend himself at his two trials? Why did he not call upon any witnesses? Why did Jesus want to be crucified? The theory of Jesus as a rebel does not tell us about the Jesus who made messianic headlines.

To answer these questions, we will continue our quest for the historical Jesus and, with yet a different set of scholars, survey the fourth face of Jesus—that of the messianic engineer who masterminded his own destiny through the fulfillment of his own predictions.

Chapter 6

The Masterminding of
a Crucifixion

In the first three portraits, Jesus was the apparent victim of fate, Jews, and Romans. In this fourth scenario—Jesus as the engineer of his own messiahship—he was not the victim but the motivator, the master chessplayer who moved Jews and Romans with great finesse to achieve his own predicted goals.

The concept of Jesus at the helm of his own destiny, planning a course of action from his baptism to his death, is not one invented by modern scholars. It is authenticated by the highest possible authority, Jesus himself. Such a scenario is outlined in all four Gospels. But, because it is so forthrightly stated, it is hidden from immediate perception unless pointed out, like the nakedness of the emperor in Hans Christian Andersen's fairy tale. As the dramatist William Congreve said, "Naked is the best disguise."

Why would Jesus have planned such a scenario? Place yourself in his sandals. If Jesus was convinced that he was the messiah, how could he convince others?

Christians should have more understanding of Jewish skepticism of the messiahship of Jesus, and Jews should have more sympathy for the Christian predicament, because someday both may again be faced with the same messiah problem they had two thousand years ago. Christians believe the messiah arrived with Jesus but that he will come a second time. Jews believe the messiah has not yet arrived but that he will come in the future. The problem for both will be how to recognize their respective messiahs when they do arrive. To further complicate matters, what if the Christian and Jewish messiahs are one and the same person? Will both Jews and Christians accept him, or will both reject him? Or will only segments of Christians or Jews accept him and the majority reject the arrival of such a self-proclaimed messiah?

The main problem for Christians, however, would be how to recognize Jesus if he were to come a second time? Could such a returned Jesus be able to convince the Christian world that he indeed was the savior come back according to Gospel prophecy? What wonders would he have to perform, what signs of divinity would he have to reveal before Christians—Catholic and Protestant— would acknowledge him?

Jesus did not have as difficult a task in Jerusalem two thousand years ago as he might have in Rome, Paris, London, or New York today. Fortunately for Jesus, the Jewish prophets had seemingly dropped many hints about the circumstances under which the first messiah would appear. If someone arrived in those days who fulfilled all those prophecies, that would constitute proof positive that such an individual was the messiah.

What were some of the prerequisites for a messiahship the evangelists say were prescribed by the prophets? In addition to having to be born in Bethlehem, and being a descendant of King David, the messiah would also have to be anointed by a prophet, enter Jerusalem on the colt of an ass, be denounced by a high priest, stand silent before his accusers, be betrayed by a most trusted friend, be mocked with gall and vinegar, die between two outcasts, rise on the third day after his death, and many other conditions. The Gospel writers assert that these and all other prerequisites in the Old Testament were fulfilled in Jesus and therefore prove his messiahship. The necessity for the fulfillment of these prophecies gives us our first glimmer of the logic behind Jesus' four predictions.

Do sentences torn out of context from the Old Testament, which the evangelists assert are validations for the messiahship of Jesus, actually pertain to Jesus? Historically they do not, say Jewish biblical scholars. These utterances in the Old Testament, quoted by the Gospel writers, were used allegorically by Hebrew patriarchs, kings, and prophets, but not with Jesus in mind.

This practice of the evangelists of pouring Old Testament wine in New Testament bottles to prove their point was a brilliant parallelism borrowed from the Jews. The Jewish scribes who had invented the method were adept at citing unrelated sentences in Hebrew Scriptures to prove that their assertions in the new Oral Law* were mandated by God Himself.

Nevertheless, how did it happen that all events in the life of Jesus as portrayed in the Gospels correspond ac-

---

*The Oral Law was a body of interpretations based on deductions from sentences in the Old Testament. Later, this Oral Law was enshrined in a body of work known as the Talmud, for which divine origin is also claimed.

curately to every hint presumably dropped by kings and prophets three hundred to a thousand years before his birth? Were they coincidental? Did God arrange events so as to fulfill each prophecy? Or did Jesus himself, in a sincere belief that he was the messiah, arrange events so that the Old Testament prophecies were fulfilled in him? And did the evangelists later fill in those prophecies Jesus himself could not have arranged for—like the virgin birth, the journey to Bethlehem, the flight to Egypt, and so on? These last two suppositions were the view held by most of the eighteenth-century German Protestant theologians.

Thus, if following the prophetic guidelines for messiahship in the Old Testament worked for Jesus, then in the eyes of his followers he was the right man in the right place at the right time to assume the glory and the burden of a messiah. Most scholars who believe in the theory that Jesus engineered his own messiahship feel that duplicity played no part in his decision to follow the "prescribed" messianic road. Just the contrary, they say. It took great faith and courage, for Jesus knew that this road would end at the cross.

Like skilled mystery writers, the evangelists reveal clues only as the "plot" progresses. It is done with such consummate deftness that one constantly has to ask oneself whether the evangelists structured this plan for Jesus or whether they faithfully recorded a plan devised by God or Jesus. Whoever originated it, the success of this messianic plan hinges on the success of six key events: Jesus must be anointed by a prophet; be proclaimed the messiah; raise someone from the dead; be betrayed by a trusted friend; be arrested by the Jews and tried by the Romans; be crucified and rise on the third day.

For the successful execution of each key point we will see Jesus be aided by six most picturesque individuals—an apocalyptic preacher named John the Baptist, a fainthearted disciple named Peter, a wealthy landowner named Lazarus, a vilified disciple named Judas, a member of the Sanhedrin named Joseph of Arimathea, and a putative prostitute named Mary Magdalene.

The first prophecy to be fulfilled was a difficult one to engineer, yet without it Jesus could not have launched his messianic career. He had to be baptized (or anointed) by Elijah, as foretold by the Jewish prophets. But how could this be? Elijah had been dead for over eight hundred years!

Luck was with Jesus. A "risen" Elijah was rumored to dwell in the vicinity of the Jordan River. Perhaps it was this very coincidence that provided the impetus for his messiahship.

Throughout the centuries, Elijah came to be thought of as the prophet who would reappear to reveal who the messiah would be. Rumors about how Elijah would appear were numerous. Some thought he would come in the guise of a young innocent boy, others that he might arrive in a cloud from heaven. Still others were convinced that the spirit of Elijah would descend upon the messiah on the wings of a white dove.

Reality was more incredible. The fulfillment of this particular prophecy came in the person of John the Baptist, a hermitlike dweller in the Judean desert. Wearing a garment of camel hair with a leather girdle just like that which Elijah himself had worn, he preached near the River Jordan, at the very spot where Elijah was said to have ascended to heaven eight centuries previously. Whether all this was sheer coincidence, or whether John

91

the Baptist made that self-identification with Elijah, or whether the evangelists spun this likeness to match faith to prophecy, cannot be historically ascertained.

John the Baptist, a weird embodiment of the apocalyptic beliefs of his time, delivered his sermons of doom with all the fire of the prophets of old. Figuratively, his stentorian voice was heard over all the land. Terror-stricken sinners flocked to the shores of the Jordan to be baptized and saved by this Jewish baptizer. And as he cried the refrain from Isaiah, "Prepare the way of the Lord . . . and all flesh shall see the salvation of God," he also proclaimed that he was awaiting the messiah.

The decisive moment was at hand. Yet, the coming encounter was fraught with danger. Why should he, Jesus, if he was the messiah, have to be baptized by someone inferior to him? And even if he were baptized by John, would prophecy be fulfilled? Yet, this baptism was demanded by prophecy, and Jesus felt impelled to go to the Jordan River to judge for himself.

It went well. According to Matthew, the moment John beheld him, he humbly acknowledged Jesus as the messiah, saying, "I need to be baptized by you, and yet you come to me." Jesus answered diplomatically, "Let it be so for now, for thus it is fitting for us to fulfill prophecy." Hearing these gracious words, John baptized Jesus.

Luke, however, was dissatisfied with Matthew's account. In his view, Jesus should not be the humble supplicant. To make sure there would be no doubt as to who was superior to whom, Luke had the unborn John the Baptist leap for joy in his mother's womb when he recognized the child in Mary's womb as that of Jesus.*

From a theological viewpoint, the first prophecy has

---

*Luke 1:44.

92

been fulfilled. After his baptism came his forty days of wrestling with the temptations of Satan in the wilderness, after which a victorious Jesus returned to Galilee. Symbolically, Jesus had wrestled with himself—a theological Hamlet faced with the decision to take or not to take the hazardous messianic road leading to death on the cross.

If his baptism had been a first step in the sequence for achieving messiahship, it was successful. From now on, masterminding the fulfillment of subsequent prophecies was paramount. Each new action was accompanied by an appropriate prophecy from the Old Testament to justify it.

What should his next move be? He must become known and be talked about as a messiah, for in the words of Oscar Wilde, "There is only one thing worse than being talked about and that is not being talked about." To get himself talked about Jesus began healing and performing wonders. This also fulfilled a prophecy by Isaiah that the "suffering servant" of God would take "our infirmities and bear our diseases."

Jesus also began to speak in parables. When asked why, he frankly stated that he did so to fulfill the prophecy that the messiah would "utter in parables what has been hidden since the foundation of the world."

About a year slipped by; the fame of Jesus grew. People were talking about him, his healings, his wonders, his sermons. The time had come for him to implement the second step in the presumed plan—to reveal his identity as the messiah. It is at this point that Jesus made his nearly fatal mistake, announcing in his hometown that he was the messiah. His family thought he had lost his mind and the townspeople wanted to throw him down a ravine. We saw him barely escape with his life.

This incident had a traumatic effect on Jesus. After

weeks of seemingly desultory wanderings in Galilee and Judah, he and his disciples arrived at Caesaria Philippi, the new scene for unveiling a second time the second key point—to be proclaimed "the Christ."

It was here that Jesus decided on a great gamble. He would disclose his messiahship and his future fate to his disciples. But this time, instead of Jesus himself announcing that he was the messiah as he did in Nazareth, he maneuvered Peter into guessing that he was the Christ. This he did with consummate skill.

First, Jesus turned to his disciples and casually asked, "Who do men say the son of man is?"★

The replies are interesting. Some said they thought he was John the Baptist, others that he was this or that prophet. But Jesus shook his head at all replies. Turning to Simon Peter, he asked: "But who do you say I am?"★★

Peter, who had seen Jesus shake his head at all other answers, came up with the right one. "You are the Christ, the son of the living God,"† he blurted out.

In the theological circles this guess is known as "Peter's confession," as though he had come across this knowledge in some mysterious way, perhaps from God Himself, and then confessed it to Jesus.

The reply of Jesus is a masterpiece of implanting positive thinking. So that the other disciples would not think it was he himself who had revealed it to Peter, Jesus said: "Blessed are you, Simon Peter. For flesh and blood have not revealed this to you, but my Father who is in heaven" (Luke 9:21–27). In other words, Jesus said that "God revealed it."

★Mark 8:31–39.
★★Mark 8:31–39.
†Matthew 16:21–18.

To make certain that Peter's identification of him as "the Christ" would not be lost on the other eleven disciples, Jesus repeated Peter's disclosure by warning them not to tell anyone that he is "the Christ."

As we have seen, it is here at Caesaria Philippi that Jesus unveiled for the first time his four predictions. "Behold," said Jesus, "we are going to Jerusalem, and the son of man will be delivered to the priests and the scribes, and they will condemn him to death, and the priests and the scribes will deliver him to the Gentiles"★ (that is, to the Romans).

Pausing for dramatic effect, Jesus revealed his next two predictions: The Romans, he said, "will mock the son of man, spit upon him and crucify him."★★ Then Jesus stated the coda, the finale, the fourth prediction: "And after three days He [Jesus] will rise again."

The disciples were stunned. This was a completely new scenario to them. Only Simon Peter dared to speak. "God forbid, Lord," he exclaimed. "This shall never happen to you."

Having blessed Peter but a few minutes ago, he now vented his anger upon him with words usually reserved for scribes and Pharisees. "Get thee behind me, Satan," he said. "You are a hindrance to me; for you are not on the side of God, but of men."†

The disciples were cowed by this outburst, and there

★Matthew 20:18–19.

★★Only in Matthew does Jesus specifically state he has to die by crucifixion. John does it inferentially; he avers that the Jews had to turn him over to the Romans to be crucified so that "This was to fulfill the word which Jesus had spoken to show by what death he wās to die." (John 18:31–32). Though Mark and Luke affirm that Jesus predicted his own death, they do not specify that death by crucifixion until later.

†Matthew 16:23.

was no further discussion. But they seemed neither pleased nor convinced. Twice more Jesus would make the same predictions, but with equally dismal results. The disciples who witnessed the rebuke of Peter kept mum, fearful of another outburst. But it is apparent they were still not convinced. Luke ascribed it to their stupidity in these blunt words: "But they [the disciples] understood none of these things; his sayings were hid from them, and they did not grasp what was said."*

Though the incident at Caesari Philippi served the purpose of identifying Jesus as "the Christ" and briefing the apostles on what to expect, we see them, nevertheless, remain unconvinced. Something more dramatic was needed. It is at this point that John introduced the miracle of miracles—the raising of Lazarus, not found in the first three Gospels. Though we have already touched briefly on Lazarus, we must now examine his function in this resurrection drama.

Mary and Martha, sisters of Lazarus, sent a message to Jesus urging him to come to Bethany right away to save their brother from death. When Jesus received it, he made a startling long-distance diagnosis. "This illness will not end in death," he told his disciples. Then he added a cryptic sentence: "This has come . . . to bring glory to the Son of God."

Why should this be so? Why should the illness of Lazarus be to the "greater glory" of Jesus? How could he gain by it?

After a wait of several days, Jesus abruptly made an aboutface. He seemingly had made a wrong prognosis, and so announced to his disciples that Lazarus was dead

---

*Luke 9:45.

after all. Then he said: "I am glad not to have been there. It will be for your good and for the good of your faith; let us now go to him."*

Did Jesus deliberately misdiagnose Lazarus's illness so that he could raise him from the dead and impress the disciples? This is the opinion of the editor of *The Abingdon Bible Commentary*, who states: "Either Jesus did not anticipate the death or else he deliberately failed to respond to the summons of Martha because he was planning a post-resurrection drama to shore up the faith of his followers."

When Jesus and his party reached Bethany, Mary led Jesus to her brother's tomb, a cave with a great stone barring its entrance. Jesus ordered it rolled away, but Martha objected. "Lord," she said, "by this time he stinks, for he has been dead four days."

Nevertheless, the stone was moved aside; Jesus lifted his eyes to heaven and said, "Father, I thank thee that thou hast answered me. I know that thou hearest me always, but I have said this on account of the people standing by, that they may believe that thou didst send me." Then, in a loud voice, he cried out, "Lazarus, come out." Lazarus did so, hands and feet still bound with bandages, and his face wrapped in cloth. Jesus said, "Unbind him and let him go."

What is the purpose of this miracle? The seeming callousness and self-aggrandizing words of Jesus have troubled many theologians. "Did John try to outdo the three synoptic evangelists by having a miracle performed on an individual four days dead and already stinking from putrefaction?" asks *The Abingdon Bible Commentary* edi-

---

*The story of Lazarus is found in John 11:1–44.

tor. "He is the only one to record the miracle of Lazarus, a miracle so incredible that it could hardly have escaped the attention of Paul, Mark, Matthew, and Luke had it really happened. Why did they not make mention of this miracle?"

In another few weeks it is Jesus who will be placed in a tomb with a huge stone rolled in front of it, though it will be angels, according to Gospel accounts, who roll the stone away, and it will be Jesus who is raised. With the Lazarus story, does John in essence tell future doubting Thomases among pagan converts—if Jesus could raise Lazarus, certainly God could raise Jesus?

Whichever way this miracle happened, the messianic road to Jerusalem was now open. With his triumphant entry into that city to the cries of hosannas and a hail of palm branches, Jesus knew there was no turning back. By accepting the plaudits of the people, by stimulating and encouraging the cries of "Hosanna, son of David," Jesus made himself guilty of treason against Rome and thus a candidate for crucifixion. But he had to avoid being arrested by the Romans at this time so that he could first be denounced by the chief priests and scribes. That is the order of events prescribed by the prophets, and that is the order of events Jesus, according to the Gospels, precipitated.

Did Jesus really manipulate events toward a predetermined goal, or did events impel him toward an end that coincided with his predictions? Two British theologians, Edwyn Hoskyns and Noel Davey, standing halfway between these two positions, have this to say:

> Jesus acted as he did and said what he did say because
> he was consciously fulfilling the necessity imposed

upon him by God through the demand of the Old
Testament. He died in Jerusalem, not because the Jews
hounded him thither and did him unto death, but because he was persuaded that, as messiah, he must journey to Jerusalem in order to be rejected and die.★

Hoskyns and Davey, however, reject the actions of Jesus
as acts of human will and ascribe them to the workings
of God. But where Hoskyns and Davey fear to tread,
other scholars wade in. Rejecting God as the motivator,
they substitute Jesus.

The stage is now set for the fourth step in the plan,
the entry of Judas Iskariot, the most enigmatic, and perhaps the most maligned, personality in the Gospels. Who
was this Judas who has gone down in history as the prototype for an unscrupulous betrayer?★★

According to the synoptic Gospels, the role of Judas
was to betray Jesus and to identify him with a kiss to the
arresting party. But why would Judas have to "betray"
Jesus? scholars ask. Mark gives no explanation. Matthew
attributes it to greed—a hunger for thirty pieces of silver.
Luke states it was because Satan entered into Judas. John
trumps them all—he equates Judas with Satan himself.†
None of these explanations satisfies.

★Hoskyns and Davey, *Riddle of the New Testament*. Faber and
Faber, London, 1931.

★★Mark 6:3 and Matthew 13:55.

†Oscar Cullman, in his work *God and Caesar* (Westminster
Press, Philadelphia, 1950), gives yet another explanation. Judas
realized, says Cullman, before the other disciples did, that Jesus
was going to defect from the Zealot cause for a messianic
priority. Disillusioned, Judas in turn betrayed Jesus. To Judas,
says Cullman, Jesus was a social traitor who was leading the
Jewish patriots down a false path.

There was no need for Judas to identify Jesus, with or without a kiss, since everybody knew him on sight. John, realizing this, has no "Judas kiss" in his Gospel. Jesus himself also realized this. When arrested, he said, "Day after day I sat in the Temple preaching and you did not seize me." What then was the role of Judas in this messianic drama?

It is the Gospel writers themselves who give us the motive for the presumed betrayal. It is from them that we learn that Jesus entrusted to Judas one of the most difficult tasks in his entire career, a task that could be fulfilled only by someone who loved Jesus as a brother, beyond life and honor. Jesus, according to the Gospel narratives, depended on Judas to betray him in order to help him fulfill three crucial prophecies, essential to his drive for messiahship. These three prophecies were: "Yes, my own familiar friend in whom I trust . . . has lifted up his heel against me" (Psalms 41:9); "For it was not any enemy that reproached me . . . but it was thou, my equal, my companion, my familiar friend" (Psalms 55:12–13); and "If you think good, give me my price . . . so they weighted for my price thirty pieces of silver" (Zechariah 11:12).

The notion of Judas as a "coconspirator" of Jesus is so subtly stated in the Gospels it is easy to miss, like a surprise check in a chess game, hidden from immediate perception until sprung. The clue is divulged at the Last Supper, where Jesus and Judas acted out a remarkable scene. At the end of the meal, Jesus gave Judas a clear signal that the time had come to betray him. He turned to his disciples and stated his purpose, plainly and clearly, leaving no doubt it had been prearranged between him and Judas:

"I am not speaking for all," said Jesus. "I know whom
I have chosen so that Scripture may be fulfilled . . . I
tell you this now, before it takes place, that when it
does take place you may believe that I am he. . . .
Truly, truly, I say to you, one of you will betray me."

(John 13:18–21)

To paraphrase his words into even-simpler English,
Jesus was saying in essence: "Look, I have chosen one of
you here to betray me because the prophets have said that
the messiah will be betrayed by a friend. I am telling you
this now, so that when I am betrayed by one of you, my
trusted friends, you will know for sure that I am the
messiah in whom prophecy has been fulfilled."

The disciples, puzzled about whom he meant, looked
at one another, and one of them asked, "Lord, who is
it?" Whereupon Jesus answered: "It is he to whom I shall
give this morsel when I have dipped it."

Jesus dipped the morsel, gave it to Judas, and said,
"What you are going to do, do quickly."

Judas, faithful to his master, set out accomplish what
Jesus had asked of him—to fulfill prophecy by arranging
for Jesus' arrest. This is the plain meaning of the text.
But because it is so plainly stated, many refuse to believe
it means what it says. "Naked is the best disguise."

The moment Judas left, Jesus turned to his disciples
and said, "Now the son of man is glorified." Why should
this betrayal "glorify" Jesus? Is it the next link in the
chain of events leading to the cross?

Most paintings of the Last Supper show either Jesus
alone with a halo or Jesus and only eleven of his twelve
disciples with such halos. Because of his supposed be-

trayal of Jesus, Judas is denied one. However, in the Prado Museum in Madrid, a painting of the Last Supper by Francesco Bassano (1550–92) shows only two individuals with halos—Jesus and Judas. So there would be no mistake about his intent, the painter also inscribed the chair with the name "Judas." Did this sixteenth-century painter divine the real meaning of Judas' action and the true sacrifice he made for Jesus and thus honor him with a halo?

It is also of interest to note that medieval artists generally did not conceive of Judas as a heinous villain. As if also divining the prophetic role of Judas in the furtherance of Jesus' messianic goal, they did not depict him as a satanic figure or a pre-Dickensian Uriah Heep, but sketched him with the same reverence as the other eleven apostles.

A second Gospel clue that shows Judas as "betraying" his lord only at the request of Jesus himself came a few hours later in the Garden of Gethsemane, the appointed place for the "betrayal," where Jesus and his disciples went after the Last Supper. "Behold, the hour is at hand and the son of Man is betrayed into the hands of sinners," said Jesus, even before he saw Judas approaching.

The entrance was timed to perfection; the action that followed was swift. Judas came toward Jesus with an armed Roman cohort. He kissed Jesus. Simon Peter drew his sword and cut off the ear of a member of the arresting party. Jesus touched the wound, and the ear grew back. He ordered Simon Peter to sheathe his sword. "Let Scripture be fulfilled," he commanded. "All this has taken place so that Scripture of the prophets might be fulfilled," he explained.* Could anything more plainly state that Jesus was consciously (or by divine inspiration) following a blueprint for a messianic crown?

---

*John 18:1–11.

John's Gospel adds another interesting corroborative note. The Roman soldiers, says John, were reluctant to arrest Jesus. When they found out who he was, "they drew back and fell to the ground," says John. This unanticipated action forced Jesus to order the soldiers to arrest him, so prophecy could be fulfilled.

Love and hate are often mirrors of distortion, and theology, like history, has little difficulty in heaping praise or abuse as needed on the wrong persons in spite of the plain meaning of the text itself. Two examples illustrating this duality are the stories of Jacob and Esau in the Old Testament and Peter and Judas in the New.

Though the text of Genesis plainly shows that Jacob not only was lazy, hanging around the tent all day, but also cheated his brother of his birthright, and though the text also shows that Esau was the breadwinner who supported a blind father, a conniving mother, and a deceitful brother, a whole series of apologetic theologians have managed to convince readers that Esau was the bad son and Jacob the good one.

We have a similar situation with Peter and Judas. Peter, who denied Jesus three times and fled his post in the hour of danger, is extolled, whereas Judas, who paid with his honor and life for serving Jesus, is vilified.

This Jacob–Esau syndrome is also found in John's Gospel in the story of Mary, sister of Lazarus, washing the feet of Jesus with an expensive perfume. When Judas rebuked her for that extravagance, asking why that perfume could not have been sold and the money given to the poor, Jesus retorted: "Let her alone. The poor you will always have with us, but you will not always have me."

Some people might be inclined to praise Judas for his compassion for the poor. As if to forestall just such a reaction, John proceeds to further vilify Judas by adding: "This Judas said, not that he cared for the poor but because he was a thief, and as he had the money box he used to take what was put into it."*

Mark, Matthew, and Luke contradict John's account. In the Gospels of Mark and Matthew this incident does not take place at the home of Lazarus but occurs at the house of Simon the Leper; it is not Mary who washes the feet of Jesus, but an unknown woman; and it is not Judas who rebukes Jesus but the other disciples.

Luke has yet a third version. He says the incident took place at the home of a Pharisee friend, that it was a whore who washed the feet of Jesus, and that Judas was not even present.** Mark, Matthew, and Luke do not accuse Judas of being a thief; only John does.

With his arrest at Gethsemane, the fifth station in the drama, Jesus was confronted with a double challenge. He had to finesse first an arrest before the Sanhedrin and then a trial before Pilate.

But why does the scenario call for such a double exposure?

The answer is simple, if one takes the "master plan" seriously. Jesus had to be tried first before the high priest to fulfill the prophecy in Isaiah that the messiah had to be "delivered by scribes and priests." Then, the "plan" called for him to be tried by Pilate, not in order to fulfill yet another prophecy, but perhaps in order for him to fulfill his own prediction that he would be crucified.

But why did death have to be through crucifixion? Why had Jesus repeatedly predicted that his death had to be through that mode of execution? He stated this most plainly in Matthew 26:3—"You know that Passover is

*John 12:6.
**Luke 7:37–39.

coming and the son of Man will be delivered up to be crucified."

But why? Why must the death he predicted for himself be by crucifixion? If we believe there is a blueprint for action, then there had to be a definite reason for it.

Jewish death sentences were swift and final. Stoning, hanging, strangling, and burning brought about certain death, rendering a manmade "resurrection" impossible. But a Roman crucifixion left a chance to escape. How could that be?

Crucifixion was a mode of punishment adopted by the Romans from the Persians. It represented the acme of the sadist's art, atrocious physical suffering, a bruised body lacerated by a scourging preceding the crucifixion, exposure to the added torture of the elements, the ignominy of a crowd watching the helpless agony of a living corpse. This punishment was considered so shameful by the Romans that it was inflicted only on rebellious slaves and seditious subject people, as already noted. Roman citizens who committed treason were beheaded.

No man could carry the complete cross because of its weight, even though Christian artists do show Jesus doing so. Only the crossbeam, placed on the condemned man's neck, had to be carried. The condemned individual was usually led naked to the place of execution, where the crossbeam was secured to a vertical stake to form a cross. The victim was then either nailed or bound to it, depending upon what type of death was desired. If a quick, merciful death was to be granted, then the hands and feet were nailed to the cross. But if a long, lingering, painful death was the object, as was usually the case, the hands were bound to the crossbar and the feet bound to a supportive *pedulum* (horizontal bar), which was nailed to the vertical stake. The body was left to rot on the cross, as an additional sign of disgrace. Vultures usually finished the work.

There are no accurate criteria to judge how long a man could survive on the cross but three to four days were the norm if the arms and feet were bound instead of nailed. The literature of the times notes many instances of individuals surviving if taken off the cross within twenty-four hours. Josephus mentions a case where he personally was permitted to take down three crucified men after a day's ordeal on the cross. Two subsequently died, but one survived. On this time factor, say scholars of this theory, hinged Jesus' chances for survival.

Did Jesus count on the fact that statistically it was more likely that he would be bound to the cross instead of nailed to it? That gamble could be one factor in the plan to escape death. But there was also another crucial factor.

The Jews were the only people in the Roman Empire who had been able to wring a concession from the Romans—that no Jew would be allowed to hang on the cross over the Sabbath. Could this be why Jesus chose a Thursday night for his arrest, reasoning that if he were crucified on a Friday morning his body would have to be taken down before sundown, before the Sabbath began? Thus, he would spend no more than six hours on the cross and could survive. This, the Gospels tell us, was exactly what happened.

The closing phase of the drama commenced. Everything had worked thus far according to script, if there was one. Judas had done an outstanding job in timing the arrest; the chief priests arrested Jesus, held a hearing, and handed him over to the Romans exactly as predicted. The trial before Pilate was next on the agenda. In this scenario, was Pilate as much the instrument of the will of Jesus as was Judas?

Pilate had to sentence Jesus to death by crucifixion if the prediction of Jesus was to work out. As only the Romans could crucify, we saw the Jews forced into turning Jesus over to the Romans.

If there is any doubt in anyone's mind that this was exactly what Jesus had in mind, John dispels that doubt by stating categorically that, "This was to fulfill the word which Jesus had spoken to show by what death he was to die" (18:32).

We saw Pilate oblige Jesus in his death wish by condemning him to the cross. The Roman soldiers scourged Jesus and walked him to Golgotha. He now reached a point of no return.

There were two problems connected with the last phase of this scenario. The first was crucial. The only way Jesus could be taken off the cross alive was if the Romans thought he was dead. The second concern was the burial. Once he was pronounced dead he would have to be taken off the cross and carried to a safe place where he could recover from his ordeal.

The "plan," if there was one, was daring. It was mad. But if Jesus was the messiah, it would have to work. Certainly God would not have permitted it to work thus far if Jesus had not been the chosen one.

Jesus had put his trust in the Old Testament prophecies; in them he found what he might have thought ample justification to believe that God would not sentence him to death but keep him alive.

Was it not written in Scripture, "Though I shall walk in the midst of trouble, you, God, will revive me" (Psalm 138:7). And was it not also written, "God shall redeem my soul from the grasp of the grave" (Psalm 30:3). And did not the Prophet Hosea prophesy: "After two days will He revive us; and on the third day he will raise us up that we may live in His sight" (Hosea 6:1–2).

There is also a pattern in Jewish history that holds up a twofold image of the Jewish hero—that of first suffering an initial humiliation, then entering into glory. Thus Joseph was first sold into slavery, then lofted to viceroy. Thus Moses was first a fugitive, then elevated to the role of emancipator. Thus David was first an outlaw, then anointed king.

Jesus was certainly aware of this mold of the Jewish hero. He stated it plainly. "Was it not necessary that the Christ should first suffer these things," he told his followers, "and then enter into his glory" (Luke 24:25–26).

The party of Roman soldiers escorting Jesus has arrived at Golgotha. It was nine o'clock in the morning. Jesus was raised to the cross. With him, as we have already learned, two rebels were also crucified in like manner.

Six hours of agony passed. It was now three o'clock in the afternoon, or as the Gospels express it, the "ninth hour" (Jesus was crucified on the third hour). Jesus said: "I thirst."

Was this a code phrase?

A "bystander" just happened to have a vessel full of vinegar at hand; he immediately saturated a sponge with the vinegar and raised it on a reed to the mouth of Jesus. When Jesus had inhaled or imbibed it, he bowed his head and said, "It is finished," and expired. The prophecy in Psalm 69:21 has also, wittingly or unwittingly, been fulfilled, as it is written, ". . . and in my thirst they gave me vinegar."

But something more than prophecy has been fulfilled.

Vinegar, which is a stimulant, should have revived Jesus. Instead, he seemingly died. Was he perhaps only in a coma, according to some theories, knocked out with a drug to give the semblance of death?

Now for the second step. To get Jesus off the cross before he died, the planners had to act fast. He had to be placed in a tomb, not a grave, if he were to survive. At this point entered mystery man Joseph of Arimathea, whose function it was to get Jesus off the cross quickly and into a tomb where he could get medical attention, recover, and have a safe hiding place for three days.

Who was Joseph of Arimathea? Was he the lowly sexton whose function it was to make sure that the dead were given a decent burial before sundown? Or was he a wealthy man, a member of the Sanhedrin, and a secret disciple of Jesus, as the evangelists state? In all probability, the evangelists are right, for Joseph was powerful enough to get an immediate audience with Pilate. A skeptical Pilate listened to his story that Jesus was dead after but six hours on the cross. He asked the centurion who was present at the crucifixion if this were so. When the centurion affirmed it, Pilate gave his permission to have Jesus taken down.

This is the Gospel truth only as told by the synoptic evangelists. But it is not the story told by John, who avers it was not Joseph of Arimathea who first went to Pilate, but the Jews. Concerned with all three crucified Jews, not just Jesus, the Jews asked Pilate's permission to have the legs of Jesus and the two rebels broken so that all three men could be buried at the same time before sundown.

But why would the Jews ask that the legs of the three crucified men be broken? By breaking the legs—a Roman custom known as *currifragum*—the weight of the body, no longer supported by the *pedulum*, chokes off the blood supply to the head and causes a quick, merciful death by suffocation. If this were done, the Jews could take the bodies off the cross before sundown. This would also assure Pilate that the Jews were not trying to trick him into getting the bodies off the cross while all three were still alive.

Pilate, still suspicious, however, sent two soldiers to Golgotha to check the facts. The two soldiers came, said John

> . . . and broke the legs of the first and of the other who had been crucified with him; but when they came to Jesus and saw that he was already dead, they did not break his legs. But one of the soldiers pierced his side with a spear, and at once there came out blood and water.

According to John, it was only after this episode that Joseph of Arimathea went to Pilate, asking for the body of Jesus.

Two fascinating details in John's Gospel indicate that Jesus might still have been alive on the cross. John states blood and water flowed out of the wound inflicted by the Roman soldier. But this would show that Jesus was alive, for blood does not flow out of a corpse, since there is no heartbeat to pump it.

The second detail is even more noteworthy. Scholars point out that in the original Greek manuscript, Pilate gave his permission to take down the "corpse" (in Greek *ptoma*) of Jesus, indicating he believed Jesus was dead. Joseph of Arimathea, however, asked permission to take down the "body" (in Greek *soma*) of Jesus indicating he believed Jesus to be alive. English translations use only the English word "body" both for Pilate's *ptoma* and Joseph of Arimathea's *soma*.

Joseph of Arimathea did receive permission from Pilate to take down the body of Jesus. But to survive the ordeal on the cross Jesus would need speedy medical attention. And indeed, as if following a script, Joseph of Arimathea had procured ahead of time a linen shroud with which to wrap the bruised body of Jesus and the services of Nicodemus, who brought healing spices. Events followed events with such logical and relentless precision that one is again forced to exclaim—who wrote this script—chance, God, Jesus, or the evangelists?

In biblical times Jews used coffins not for burial but only for transporting the dead to their graves, where they were laid horizontally on a bier, faceup. In ancient Palestine, the poor were buried in the ground; tombs hewn in rock were reserved for the rich. But neither the ground or a tomb was a temporary resting place; both were considered graves. To survive, Jesus could not be buried in the ground; he would have to be placed in a tomb.

Since Joseph of Arimathea was rich, we are not surprised to learn that the body of Jesus was placed in a new tomb, specifically hewn ahead of time for this occasion, implying foreknowledge.

A huge stone was rolled in front of the entrance, reminiscent of the burial place of Lazarus.

It had been a long, long Friday. It began at sunup with the trial of Jesus before Pilate and ended at sundown with his burial in a tomb by Joseph of Arimathea.

111

Saturday would be a day of silence. The Gospels tell us nothing about that day. Until now, all events predicted by Jesus, for whatever reason, had taken place. But would his last prediction also be fulfilled? Would he rise on the third day after his crucifixion?

Chapter 7

A Concerto of Faith and Doubt

Dawn Sunday morning, the third day after the crucifixion, is the cue for the entry of Mary Magdalene. She is as much the mystery woman as Joseph of Arimathea is the mystery man. She has also become almost as maligned as Judas. For some reason popes loved to depict her as a fallen woman. It was Pope Gregory (540–604) who first pinned the tag "whore" on Mary Magdalene, identifying her with the fallen woman in Luke who anointed the feet of Jesus with that expensive ointment. In common speech Magdalene has come to signify a contrite prostitute, and a Magdalene hospital is one where prostitutes are given shelter.

Actually, Mary Magdalene was a nice Jewish girl from the town of Magdala who had emotional problems. She was a hysteric, or a neurotic, or a schizoid, for the Gospels tell us Jesus had driven seven demons out of her.

In clinical terms, this drastic cure effected a strong emotional transference to Jesus, and she became one of his most devoted followers. The Gnostic gospels aver she was married to Jesus; other apocryphal literature hint of romantic liaisons. But no historical evidence exists for such suppositions.

Mary was present at Golgotha when Jesus was crucified, and she was the first one at his tomb early Sunday morning. What was she doing there?

Ernest Renan has paid Mary Magdalene a fitting tribute and supplied one possible answer—to unveil the resurrection.

> Next after Jesus she [Mary Magdalene] was the most essential part in the founding of Christianity. The image created by her vivid susceptibility still hovers before the world. She, as chief princess among visionaries, has better than any other made the vision of impassioned soul a real thing to the world's conviction. That grand cry from her woman's heart, "He is risen," has become the mainspring of faith for mankind.★

However, the evangelists do not say she was there to witness a resurrection. Mark states she came to anoint the body of Jesus. Matthew says Mary went to view the sepulcher. Luke avers she came with spices. John gives no explanation whatsoever.

Certainly Mary, being Jewish, would not have come to anoint a buried corpse or to sprinkle it with spices.

★Renan, *The Life of Jesus*. Random House, New York, 1927.

The tomb, as stated, was a grave. To disturb a body in a grave, whether in the ground or in a tomb, would have been a desecration, a heinous Jewish offense then and now, as well as in all Christendom today. What then was Mary's role?

Possibly Renan is right. Perhaps Mary's theological function was to discover that the tomb was empty, that the body of Jesus was gone, and to raise (in Renan's words) "the grand cry from her woman's heart"—"He is risen"—and thus proclaim to the world that the fourth prediction of Jesus had been fulfilled.

Time has given birth to four views of the resurrection. The first is based on faith. Whether Jesus died from the ordeal on the cross or from a spear wound is immaterial to believers. He died and he rose as testified to by those who saw him and believed in him. The fact that Jesus had predicted his resurrection is explained by saying that he was carrying out the will of God, not personally arranging for these events. Belief in a risen Jesus on the part of his followers is independent of belief in an empty tomb.

The second view, basically that of Reimarus,* rejects faith. It holds that the disciples took the body from the tomb and then spread the news of a resurrection.

The third view is a composite of the theories of those eighteenth-century German Protestant theologians who followed the lead of Reimarus. Essentially, a number of these scholars contend that Jesus did not die immediately from the wound inflicted by the spear or the ordeal on the cross but lived on for about forty days (as attested in Acts) before he died. Such a scenario, contend these scholars, would explain the resurrection accounts in the Gospels without having to resort to the supernatural. People

*Reimarus, *The Goal of Jesus and His Disciples.* E. J. Brill, Leiden, 1970.

who testified to having seen Jesus walking on earth after seeing his body on the cross would have been telling the truth. And thus, according to these theologians, Jesus realized a resurrection before he died.

The fourth view is that of the late nineteenth- and twentieth-century academics who are more objective than the German Protestant scholars and less hostile to Christianity. They see no plot on the part of the disciples, or of Joseph of Arimathea, or of Jesus himself to structure a resurrection. Because it was later interpreted that he had been resurrected in order to be accepted as a messiah does not mean that Jesus had such a novel construction of Scripture in mind. The idea of a resurrection arose, say these scholars, after the death of Jesus, to conform to the needs of the new growing faith, and then was retroactively attributed to Jesus.

The scholar greatly responsible for this fourth view was Christian Hermann Weisse (1801–66), a philosopher turned theologian. Weisse had first gained fame with his discovery that the Gospel of Mark was chronologically the first, not that of Matthew. It was he who also established the order in which the other three Gospels were written. One sentence in his account of the resurrection of Jesus could be the standard for brevity and clarity for those rejecting divine participation in the rising of Jesus. "The historical fact about the resurrection," wrote Weisse, "is only the existence of the belief."

This fourth view has been summarized eloquently in one paragraph by Renan:

Had his [Jesus'] body been taken away, or did enthusiasm, always credulous, create afterward the group of narratives by which it was sought to establish faith in the resurrection? In the absence of opposing documents this can never be ascertained. Let us say, however, that the strong imagination of Mary Magdalene played an important part in the circumstances.*

Amazingly enough, it is the evangelists themselves who give supportive evidence for this fourth view.

If we consider the concept of the resurrection as it develops chronologically in the Four Gospels—from Mark in 70 A.D. to John in 110 A.D.—an interesting sequence in four movements of doubt and faith emerges. The interplay is like a piano concerto—doubt (the orchestra) constantly raising new questions, and faith (the piano) answering the scoffers with new proof. Mark's Gospel was the first movement in this resurrection concerto, boldly making the initial statement.

History has bequeathed us two versions of Mark's last chapter dealing with the resurrection—one, the original text as written by Mark himself, and the other, an expanded ending tacked on by concerned Church Fathers a century later.

In Mark's original text (16:1–8), Mary Magdalene, accompanied by two other women, came to the tomb early Sunday morning to anoint the body of Jesus. They found the stone rolled back and upon entering the tomb were met by a youth** robed in white who told them Jesus had "risen" and would meet with his disciples at a later date. Mary and her companions "fled with trem-

---

*Renan, *The Life of Jesus.*
**Some scholars surmise that this youth dressed in white is the same youth dressed in white linen cloth who ran away naked when the Romans tried to arrest him along with Jesus (Mark 14:51).

bling" and, in the words of Mark, "said nothing to anyone for they were afraid." Here the original Gospel of Mark ends.

This is indeed an amazing ending for a saint of Mark's stature. It implies that forty years after the death of Jesus, an empty tomb held little or no significance for him. He gives no evidence of a resurrection, no account of Jesus appearing personally to Mary, and no testimony to a meeting with his disciples.

No wonder Church Fathers were perturbed by this abrupt conclusion, for it was a most unsatisfactory one to new Christian converts. There were compelling reasons for a more positive ending. It was thus that a century later, Church Fathers tacked on twelve sentences to Mark's last chapter (16:9–20) to conform to the endings of Matthew and Luke, affirming that Jesus did appear both to Mary Magdalene and to the surviving disciples.*

The orchestration of doubt began to sweep Christian communities in the decade following Mark's Gospel. Pagans considering conversion to Christianity were puzzled by Mark's abrupt ending. They wanted more proof of a resurrection.

A new generation "that did not know Jesus" asked: How do we know that a resurrection took place just because Jesus was not in the tomb? Had Jesus died on the cross or not? they asked. Who was right about the "resurrection"? Was it the Apostolic Church, which saw in Jesus an ordinary Jewish messiah not bodily resurrected, or was it Paul's version of Jesus as the "risen Christ"?

New testimony surfaced, and Matthew in Alexandria

---

*Though the *Douay* and the *King James Version*s include these extra sentences in the main text, the *Oxford Annotated Bible* relegates them to a footnote, and other versions eliminate them completely.

and Luke in Antioch, who composed their Gospels within ten to fifteen years of each other, incorporated these new scores of faith in them.

To counteract the persistent rumors in the early Christian world that the disciples had stolen the body of Jesus and then spread the news that Jesus had risen, Matthew executed a brilliant checkmate by shifting the suspicion from the disciples to the Jews (27:62–66; 29:11–15). Matthew stated that the chief priests asked Pilate to post guards at the tomb for three days so the disciples would not be able to steal the body and claim that he had risen. Pilate granted permission. Sunday morning, a male angel descended from heaven and rolled away the stone. Trembling with fear, the guards ran to tell the priest what had happened. But the priests bribed the guards to tell the people that the disciples had stolen the body, and, said Matthew, "This is the story the Jews have been spreading to this day."

But Matthew was mistaken. It was not the Jews who told this story but the Gnostic Christians, and later, Church Fathers like Tertullian, and German Protestant scholars like Reimarus.

Matthew also transformed the youth dressed in white in Mark's account to an angel, and Luke made it two angels. Both Matthew and Luke testified that Jesus appeared in person to Mary Magdalene. In Matthew, Jesus appeared to his disciples but once to testify to his own resurrection, but in Luke Jesus made two such appearances.

In both Matthew and Luke, Jesus reminded his disciples of his predictions and how they were fulfilled in him so men might believe. But it was only Luke who, for the first time, had Jesus tell his disciples to please examine the nailholes in his hands to verify that he was the one who was crucified. (Thus far, none of the three synoptic evangelists has mentioned a spear wound.)

Despite the new testimony of Matthew and Luke, the concerto of doubt continued to swell. By the end of the first century A.D., the Christian diaspora embraced the entire Roman world. By this time, too, most new Christian converts were former pagans inasmuch as Jews no longer flocked to Christian tabernacles under the misapprehension that they were renovated tents of Jacob.

As more and more pagans embraced the Christian faith, they also infected the Christian body with more and more esoteric varieties of heresy. One Christian splinter sect claimed that John the Baptist was the true messiah who unwittingly had baptized a false one in Jesus. Another group believed that whoever had carried the cross was the one who was crucified. Since Mark, Matthew, and Luke had stated that Simon of Cyrene had carried the cross for Jesus, this sect held that it was Simon, not Jesus, who had died on the cross and that Jesus was still alive.

The most vexing challenge, however, was the persistent question—how did Mark, Matthew, and Luke know that Jesus was dead when he was taken off the cross? Daily experience with the Roman crucifiers had shown that one did not usually die on the cross in only six hours. More proof was demanded.

John was aware of these heresies swirling around in Christian circles. Composing his Gospel in Ephesus, he incorporated the latest tenets of faith of the expanding Christian creed, which countered the doubts raised in the wake of these heresies. John the Baptist was denigrated in his Gospel and compelled to declare publicly that he was not the Christ, that he was not even a prophet but only a lowly messenger, not worthy of tying Jesus' sandals.

To nullify the heretic view that Simon, not Jesus, was the messiah, John bluntly stated that Jesus carried his own cross. John was also the first to include in his testament the new oral tradition about a spear wound in the side to explain Jesus' quick death on the cross.*

In John's Gospel, Jesus made three postcrucifixion visits to his disciples. In the first, he showed them not only the nailholes in his hands (as in Luke) but also the spear wound in his side. When the disciple Thomas, who was not present, was informed of that visit, he said, "Unless I see in his hands the print of nails, and place my hand in his side, I will not believe." It was this cynicism that earned him the sobriquet "Doubting Thomas." Jesus returned for the second visit to convince Thomas, saying, "Put your finger here and see my hands; and put your hand and place it at my side; do not be faithless but believing." In the third manifestation to his apostles at Lake Tiberias, Jesus forecasted a possible Second Advent—that is, a Second Coming—which closes the Gospel of John.

As doubts about the spear wound nevertheless persisted in spite of John's testimony, three intrepid Church Fathers came to the rescue. Justin Martyr (circa 100–67)

---

*The fact that John was the only evangelist to have anything to say about a spear wound worried the early Church Fathers. To remedy this omission, some Church Fathers inserted a corroborative sentence in the Gospel of Matthew that read: "And another took a spear and pierced his side, and there came out water and blood." The prose style of this sentence differs markedly from the rest of Matthew. It is so patently a "pious fraud" that it has been eliminated from most English Bible texts, although some do carry that sentence in a footnote.

asserted that Jesus had died so quickly because he had not been bound but had been nailed to the cross by both his hands and feet. Tertullian (160–230?), who could always be counted on to come up with a brilliant answer, did it again. "It must be believed," he said, "precisely because it is so absurd." When that did not stem the tide of doubt, Origen (circa 185–254) issued a pronouncement that the death of Jesus on the cross after but six hours was a miracle wrought by God and therefore could not be questioned.

These *obiter dicta* by Justin, Tertullian, and Origen set the mold for Western artists to portray Jesus nailed to the cross instead of bound to it. But curiously enough, whereas Jesus is usually shown with his hands and feet nailed to the cross, as in the famed crucifixion paintings by Rubens, Mantegna, and Antonello de Messina, the two rebels crucified along with him are typically shown bound to their crosses, as if to explain visually why Jesus had died on the cross after but six hours whereas the two rebels had not.

What do these successive strata of new information in the Gospels—from Mark, to Matthew, to Luke, to John—signify? Do they constitute a form of deception, as averred by the German Protestant scholars? No, say other historians. As there was no concept of a historical Jesus in those first centuries of Christianity, their view is that the evangelists reflected the faith and belief of their times. Jesus became a messiah by popular demand, and the concept of a resurrection was born in faith and handed down by tradition.

And thus, as Renan states it, when Mary raised the cry "He is risen," she encapsulated in that cry the hopes and beliefs of a segment of the world that came to embrace the new creed that became known as Christianity.

The journey to Jerusalem is now over. We have presented four faces of Jesus, and evangelists, theologians, and historians have given their explanations as to how they think the fulfillment of the four predictions was achieved.

However, whether they have explained the fulfillment of these predictions to our complete satisfaction is still debatable. The questions of the crucifixion and resurrection still defy historical analysis, still remain an enigma embedded in faith.

We now must return to our gallery where hang our seven portraits and view the last three to see what further light they can shed on the historical Jesus and his enigmatic predictions.

Chapter 8

Did Christianity Exist
Prior to Jesus?

For the first four views of Jesus, we found the sources directly in the Gospels. For the fifth, Jesus as an Essene, we can go to the Gospels only indirectly, for nowhere in the New or Old Testament are the Essenes mentioned by name. Yet, today, many renowned scholars claim that John the Baptist was an Essene, that Jesus might have been one, that Paul was influenced by the Essenes, and that Christianity itself is a form of Essenism that succeeded.

For twenty centuries, Christians have generally believed that the concepts of Christianity were totally the innovation of Jesus, sprung from his brain like a latter-day Pallas Athena, fully clothed with the latest tenets. Jews were happy with that perception, for they wanted no credit for any Christian dogma, feeling that in contributing Jesus to the Christians, they had done enough. Fundamentalist Christians concurred with them.

Then, in the spring of 1947, on the eve of the rebirth of the State of Israel, an electrifying event occurred—the discovery of the Dead Sea Scrolls. To the mutual horror of fundamentalist Christians and Orthodox Jews, these Scrolls revealed not only a Jewish prototype for Jesus a century or so before he was born but also an outline for a future Christianity. They revealed that most of the rites derided by Jews as "claptrap" and lauded by Christians as "uniquely Christian" had been conceived and practiced by a sect of Jews a century or two before Jesus appeared on the scene.

No fiction writer would have dared to invent the circumstances under which the scrolls were found or what they contained. The discovery was made accidentally by an illiterate black-marketeer—a teenage Bedouin with the fierce name of Muhammed the Wolf—as he stealthily crossed the Arab-Israeli battle lines with a flock of contraband sheep and goats to be sold on the black market in—of all places—Bethlehem.

In the spring of 1947, Palestine was in crisis. The defunct League of Nations Mandate over Palestine was about to end. The British, who had administered that Mandate since the end of World War I, were preparing to leave the following spring. The Arabs were promising to invade any future independent state of Israel the moment the British left.

Having no forewarning that they would be ignominiously defeated in this and four other wars with Israel, the Arabs prepared for their invasion of Palestine with confidence. Practicing for "that day," the Arabs started sniping at the Jews, and the Jews returned their fire. As the British sided with the Arabs, the Jews also sabotaged the British to hasten their departure. The British hanged Jewish freedom fighters, and the Jews reciprocated by hanging British soldiers. Palestine was a proverbial powder keg. These were trying conditions under which Muhammed the Wolf had to earn a living. To reach the lucrative black market in Bethlehem, he had to elude Arab, British, and Jewish patrols. His journey was long and arduous. Among other things, he had to float his ambulant merchandise across the Jordan River. Then there was the trek across the strip of Judean wilderness before he would reach his goal. A native of the region, he took a little-known path along the desolate, hilly, western shore of the Dead Sea. In pursuing a stray goat, Muhammed passed a cave and idly threw a stone into it. To his astonishment and fright, he heard a sound of breaking pottery. He ran away but returned the next day with a friend engaged in the same profession. Together they explored the cave.

Inside, the two amazed youths found eight still-unbroken, tall clay jars, the kind Rachel might have carried to the well where Jacob met her, or Zipporah might have used while tending her father's flock when Moses first saw her. Inside one of the jars, Muhammed and his friend found seven foul-smelling, cylindrical objects wrapped in linen and coated with a black pitch. Unrolling the linen wraps, they uncovered parchment scrolls, which turned out to be ancient documents written mostly in Hebrew. The two young Bedouins had stumbled upon a two thousand-year-old Essene *genizah**—a storage house for re-

---

*Genizah comes from the Hebrew word "hiding." Even to this day, Jews do not destroy sacred works like the Torah, the Old Testament, but deposit them in storage places where time will eventually disintegrate them.

ligious manuscripts. The two entrepreneurs took the seven scrolls with them, hoping to make a few shekels.

As it was, a "few shekels" was all they got for their find, although it contained five most important, hitherto unknown, documents, now entitled *Manual of Discipline*, *Habakkuk Commentary*, *The War of the Sons of Light with the Sons of Darkness*, *Zadokite Fragments*, and *Book of Jubilees*.

These five scrolls would force Christianity "to abandon its claim to uniqueness and admit its doctrines, ethics, worship, and organizations were all derived from an earlier form of religious practice."* Or as Professor W. F. Allbright, America's foremost biblical archaeologist, expressed it: "The new evidence with regard to beliefs and practices of Jewish sectarians of the last two centuries B.C. bids fair to revolutionize our approach to the beginnings of Christianity."

The last two scrolls of the seven found by the two young Arab black-marketeers were two manuscripts of the Book of Isaiah—one complete, the other incomplete, but both virtually identical in text to the Book of Isaiah handed to us by time.

In Bethlehem, they took their find to a dealer in antiquities, who did not think the Scrolls had any value. They went next to a Syrian cobbler, who gave them a few silver coins in exchange for three of the documents, thinking he would use the parchment to sole shoes. On a hunch, however, he took them to a Metropolitan (same rank as an archbishop) of a Coptic monastery in Old Jerusalem. From here on the story as to who-got-what-for-how-much-from-whom gets lost in denials, contradictions, and amnesia.

*R. K. Harrison, *The Dead Sea Scrolls: An Introduction*. Harper Torchbooks, New York, 1961.

The Metropolitan did not buy the three scrolls from the cobbler but instead contacted the two Bedouin boys, who, in the meantime, had gone to see a Jewish merchant who thought of giving the remaining scrolls to Hebrew University. The Metropolitan literally scared the hell out of the boys as to what would happen to them if they were caught in the Jewish section of Jerusalem and induced them to sell their four remaining manuscripts to him for a reputed price of fifty pounds. He eventually sold them to the Jews for $250,000.

Now began the battle of the experts. The Metropolitan took the Scrolls to the Syrian Patriarch of Antioch, who did not think any parchment could be two thousand years old. Common sense told him that. Next, the Metropolitan showed them to a dealer in antiquities, in Palestine, who, after consulting his references pronounced his judgment: They were fakes. The Metropolitan now tried his luck with a Jew from New Jerusalem, but being circumcised did not confer greater wisdom upon him. His verdict was one the Metropolitan did not like at all. The documents, he said, were manuscripts stolen from a synagogue.

Meanwhile, the antique dealer in Bethlehem, whom Muhammed the Wolf had first contacted, bought the three scrolls from the Syrian cobbler and offered them for sale to Dr. E. L. Sukenik, head of the archaeology department at Hebrew University in Jerusalem. In November 1947, he and Dr. Sukenik, both defying death, faced each other across a barbed-wire fence in war-torn Jerusalem. The dealer slipped one of the scrolls to Dr. Sukenik, who recognized its authenticity. After protracted negotiations, a deal was made for the purchase of the three scrolls for an undisclosed sum, which rumor has placed at $100,000.

Another six years were to elapse before the four scrolls owned by the Metropolitan were acquired by Hebrew University. The Metropolitan came to the United States and deposited them in a safety-deposit box in a New York bank. One day in 1953, there appeared a discreet ad in the *Wall Street Journal*:

> Biblical manuscripts dating to at least 200 B.C. are for sale. This would be an ideal gift to an educational or religious institution by an individual or a group.

General Yigael Yadin of the Israeli Army, and also a famed archaeologist, was in the United States at the time and, through a third party, negotiated the purchase of the Scrolls for a quarter-million dollars. Eventually all seven manuscripts discovered by Muhammed the Wolf found their way to the Hebrew University of Jerusalem, where they are housed in a specially built shrine of steel and concrete known as "The House of the Book."

As soon as the story of the Dead Sea find was out, the biggest scroll hunt in the history of the world was launched. To date, over three hundred caves have been explored, but in just ten of these was additional material found. Only ten new manuscripts found were completely preserved, but these and thousands of scroll fragments yielded the caves' secret. The language in the scrolls and fragments is mostly Hebrew, with some Aramaic, and a smattering of Greek. At least one fragment of every book in the Old Testament was found except for the Book of Esther. Scholars believe this book was deliberately omitted by the Essene scribes because it does not mention the name of God even once. The dating of all the works discovered has been placed between 200 B.C. and 1 A.D.

In 1951 came another momentous discovery that was to shake fundamentalist Christians and Jews even more than had the Dead Sea Scrolls. A Jewish monastery was unearthed right in the heart of Qumran, as the area around the Dead Sea caves is called. A Jewish monastery! This was unbelievable. Everyone knew that only Christians had monasteries, not Jews. But a Jewish monastery it was—three centuries before the first Christian monastery was to appear in the world.

For five years the digging of this monastery went on in the terrible solitude of the Qumran landscape. Edmund Wilson has probably given it the best word description: "The landscape of the Dead Sea wilderness is monotonous, subduing, and dreadful. It is a landscape without physiognomy; no faces of gods or men; no bodies of recumbent animals are suggested by the shapes of the hills."* Another scholar, possessed of wit, added: "Nothing but monotheism could come out of this. There is no crevice for any nymph, anywhere."

But this scholar was wrong, for out of this landscape came future Christianity. Out of this landscape came John the Baptist, who baptized Jesus just two miles down the road from the monastery at the Jordan River. Two miles farther north is the Jordan Wilderness, where Jesus spent his forty days of temptation with the devil.

The discovery of the Dead Sea Scrolls and the Jewish monastery confirmed the previous belief of some scholars that a form of "Christianity" had existed at least one to two hundred years before Jesus. Most prominent among

*Wilson, *The Scrolls From the Dead Sea*. Oxford University Press, New York, 1955.

them was Ernest Renan, who in 1863 wrote: "Christianity is an Essenism which has largely succeeded."

The Essene Scrolls also revealed, to the disbelief of the Christian world, that half a century before Jesus there had existed a prototype for him. The messianic career of Jesus was modeled on someone known in the Essene creed as the "Teacher of Righteousness."

Nowhere do the Scrolls identify the people of this sect as Essenes, yet they are so known today by most scholars. The reason is that the description of this sect in the "Dead Sea" or "Qumran Scrolls" (as they are also called) is the same as that of the Essene sect in ancient Palestine described by a handful of scholars twenty centuries ago. Among them were Philo and Josephus, two Jewish scholars, and Pliny the elder, a Roman historian. Though all three gave excellent accounts of the communal life and religious practices of the Essenes, they failed to observe the uniqueness of these Essene doctrines, which separated them from the mainstream of Judaism and which eventually were to link them to an emerging Christianity.

The discoveries of the Dead Sea Scrolls and the Essene monastery were at first greeted with a thunderous silence by fundamentalist Christians and Orthodox Jews. As already noted, the fundamentalist Christians were not anxious to credit the Jews with the origin of their religion and rites, which for two millennia had been extolled as uniquely Christian. And the Orthodox Jews were not anxious to assume credit for the authorship of a creed they had rejected for twenty centuries. But when silence did not halt the dissemination of the contents of the Essene Scrolls, they both met the challenge with superb invective.

Who were the Essenes?

132

The Essenes were an obscure sect of Jews dating back to the second century B.C., who withdrew themselves from all political activities to devote their lives to religious contemplation. Thus, by the time of Jesus' ministry, they had already been separated for over a century from the larger Jewish communities to the periphery of smaller towns, much in the same way the Amish and Shakers in the United States separated themselves into their own communities.

The Essenes did not refer to themselves by that name but spoke of themselves as the "Elect of God." Their final authority was no longer the Old Testament but their own Scrolls, known to them as the "New Covenant," which by its Latin name would be the "New Testament."

The parallel between the communal life of the Essenes and the future early Christians is striking. As did the early Christians, the Essenes practiced a sort of naive communism wherein all goods were shared. The Essenes forbade both divorce and polygamy. In the words of the historian Josephus, "They rejected all pleasure as evil, but esteemed continence and conquest of passion as a virtue."

The Essene concept of purity went so far as to forbid all sexual intercourse within the walls of the holy city of Jerusalem, and defecation was forbidden on the Sabbath. Men bathed in a loincloth, and women bathed wrapped in linen. Meals were taken communally, and each community was under the stewardship of a bishop.

To preserve their celibacy, the Essene monks and priests did not marry. But those who had not attained the highest standards of purity could degrade themselves by marrying and begetting children. Most additions to the Essene community came through adoption of children from other sects, who then were trained in their ascetic ways.

133

Like the Pharisees and the future Christians, the Essenes believed in the immortality of the soul, in resurrection, in an imminent coming of the messiah. They also believed in the punishment of the wicked in an everlasting hell and reward for the good in heaven. They developed elaborate purification rites, one of which was baptism, or immersion in water for remission of sins and rebirth into a new, purer life.

The core of the Essene creed was established around 150 B.C. by a Jewish priest who could not accept the Temple hierarchy. Though the Essenes rejected the Sadducee cult of sacrifice, they nevertheless accepted the idea of priesthood and called themselves the "Sons of Zadok," the name of the high priest in the days of King Solomon. For the cult of sacrifice they substituted a ceremony all their own—a "Sacred Supper" presided over by a priest and attended by at least ten persons. This sacred meal, in which the priests blessed the bread and the wine, was a messianic ritual supper to signify the coming of the Kingdom of God.

We now come to that remarkable personality, the Teacher of Righteousness, who was as central to the Essene New Covenant as Jesus is to the Christian New Testament. His disciples viewed him as the "suffering servant of God," called from the womb "to restore the true Covenant." All who believed in him as the messiah would be healed, as stated in Isaiah, ". . . by his bruises are we healed." This was also claimed for Jesus.

The Teacher of Righteousness was a man of sorrow, destined to be slain by the "wicked priests." But he was also the instrument chosen by God for the salvation of mankind. He was the "Nazarene" (from the Hebrew word *nezer*, that is, "shoot") of the house of Jesse, the father of King David, the rock on which the future Essene

Church would be built. He was also known as "The Light," "The Spirit of Truth," and the "son of Man."

To show that prophecy had been fulfilled in him, the Teacher of Righteousness continually quoted Scriptures to prove it, just as Jesus was to do. So, for instance, when the Teacher of Righteousness was given the mission to announce the good tidings, he quoted the words from Isaiah as proof: "The Spirit of the Lord God is upon me because the Lord has anointed me to bring good tidings to the afflicted." These are the same words, as we saw, that Jesus used a century later when he announced in Nazareth that he was the messiah.

In the Essene document *The Testaments of the Twelve Patriarchs*, the Teacher of Righteousness states:

I was beset with hunger, and the Lord nourished me.
I was alone, and the Lord comforted me;
I was sick and the Lord visited me.

In Matthew we read:

For I was hungry and you gave me food,
I was a stranger and you welcomed me,
I was sick and you visited me. (25:35–36)

Which came first? The Essene gospel was composed between 200 and 100 B.C. Matthew wrote his gospel over a century later.

Who was this Teacher of Righteousness? We do not even know his name. There is much debate about the

135

exact dates of his ministry, though most scholars agree that it began sometime around 105–95 B.C. and ended about 65–55 B.C., almost a century before the crucifixion of Jesus. The scrolls do not state the exact nature of death suffered by this Teacher, but we know it was a violent one (some scholars claim it was by crucifixion) at the hands of the "wicked priest," whose name is also unknown. But, convinced that their slain Teacher would reappear among them, resurrected from the dead, his disciples thought of Qumran (at the Jordan River) as the most likely area for him to reappear. Here, in their monastery, they awaited the return of their messiah while preparing themselves for Judgment Day.

An ever-greater number of scholars now believe with Renan that Christianity is indeed a "form of Essenism which has largely succeeded." One cannot fail to perceive the remarkable similarities between Essenism and Christianity, between the Teacher of Righteousness and Jesus. This view, when first stated in a public lecture in 1950 by Dr. André Dupont-Sommer, professor at the Sorbonne, in Paris, caused a sensation in Europe.

In his lecture, Dupont-Sommer stated that although the Teacher of Righteousness was not Jesus (as some scholars claim) but a Jewish priest of the first century B.C., his life, nevertheless, closely paralleled that of Jesus. According to Professor Dupont-Sommer this Teacher of Righteousness was probably crucified and believed risen from the dead. "The Galilean Master, as He is presented to us in the writings of The New Testament," Dupont-Sommer went on to say, "appears in many respects as an astonishing reincarnation of the Teacher of Righteousness."

Is this comparison outrageous? The Teacher of Righteousness preached penitence, poverty, humility, chastity, love for one's neighbor; he was said to be the Elect, the messiah of God, the messiah-redeemer of the world; he was the object of the hostility of the priests, the party of the Sadducees; he was condemned and put to death; he founded a church whose adherents fervently awaited his glorious return.

All this was also said about or ascribed to Jesus almost two centuries later by the evangelists.

Dupont-Sommer summarizes the meaning of the resemblance succinctly:

> All these similarities . . . taken together constitute a very impressive whole. The question at once arises, to which of the two sects, the Jewish or the Christian, does priority belong? Which of the two was able to influence the other? The Teacher of Righteousness died about 65–53 B.C.; Jesus the Nazarene died about 30 A.D. In every case in which the resemblance compels or invites us to think of a borrowing, this was on the part of Christianity.*

This is not to argue that Jesus was actually the Teacher of Righteousness himself, although one renowned scholar, Professor J. T. Teicher of the University of Cambridge, has put forth such a theory. The Teacher of Righteousness, says Dr. Teicher, is no one else but Jesus, and the Wicked Priest is Saint Paul, because of his enmity to James, and his efforts to abolish the Law. One individual even more closely identified in the Gospels with the Essenes than Jesus is John the Baptist, who preached two

---

*DuPont-Sommer, *The Dead Sea Scrolls: A Preliminary Survey*. Helicon Press, Baltimore, 1958.

miles from the Essene monastery. When the Essenes referred to their dwelling place at Qumran they called it "the desert," and that is exactly what Luke does: "The word of the Lord was made unto John . . . in the desert." In the Essene *Manual of Discipline* it is written: "The men of Israel should remove themselves from the society of wicked men, into the desert, and there prepare the way, as it is written"; "Prepare the way for the Lord, make it straight in the wilderness the path of our God." That is exactly what the Gospels say that John the Baptist said and did—". . . a voice crying in the wilderness, preparing a highway for the Lord."

John was called "the Baptist" because he taught, in accordance with the Essene creed, that men could cleanse their souls symbolically through "baptism." The Gospels tell us that John subsisted on a diet of honey and locusts. Locusts were also on the Essene list of gourmet foods. One Essene scroll (the *Damascus Document*) specified that locusts must be roasted. Perhaps John roasted his locusts in the scorching desert sun, and then dipped them in honey, if these two foods were indeed all he ate.

John the Baptist's mission was, however, to await the messiah and to baptize him in fulfillment of Essene prophecy. What the Essenes awaited was the second coming of the Teacher of Righteousness; what arrived was the first advent of Jesus.

Were John and Jesus Essenes, and did, perhaps, John remain an Essene, whereas Jesus abandoned the faith after his baptism by John? This is strictly speculation, but the Gospels do hint of a subsequent enmity between John and Jesus over the essential Essene rite of baptism.

This enmity of John toward Jesus has puzzled many scholars. Did John think he had baptized the wrong person? Why the element of doubt?

This doubt is most boldly stated in the Gospel of Matthew, where John sends a message to Jesus asking: "Are you the one who is come, or are we to expect another,"* implying Jesus might be an impostor. Perhaps what worried John the Baptist was that Jesus had abandoned the rite of baptism.

Equally puzzling is Jesus' answer to John: "Go tell John what you hear and see; the blind recover their sight, the lame walk, the deaf hear, the dead are raised, and the poor are hearing the good news."**

But nowhere does Jesus say the people were baptized. The puzzle, of course, is why Jesus found it essential that he himself be baptized but did not baptize others. We have confirmation for this in the Gospel of John, which unequivocally states, "Jesus himself did not baptize."†

Was Jesus an Essene? Is he a Christian version of the Essene Teacher of Righteousness? Is Jesus' statement that he must go to Jerusalem there to fulfill his four predictions but a syndromic recapitulation of the same events we saw unfold in the life of the Teacher of Righteousness? Is Essenism the fifth face of Jesus? These are questions scholars still debate.

With Jesus dead, however, both Essenism and Christianity seemed doomed. But Christianity did succeed. Who or what rescued it from oblivion? Some say it was the force of the Galileean master himself; others say it was the guiding genius of another Jew, named Paul, who was to make Christian history by impressing a new Christian face on the Jewish Jesus—that of the Christ.

---

*Matthew 11:2.
**Matthew 11:3–6.
†John 4:2.

Chapter 9

The View from Paul's Mind

Like the Old Testament, the New Testament, too, is often unsparing in laying bare the frailties of its heroes. None of the eleven surviving apostles* showed up at the crucifixion of Jesus. Scattered to the four winds on the wings of fear, they eventually returned to Jerusalem "with great joy," according to Luke, and "were continually in the Temple blessing God." It should be emphasized that Luke does not say they were blessing Jesus. They were in the Temple with the other Jews who were offering animal sacrifices to God.

The only primary-source documents we have concerning what happened to these early Christians during the forty years between the death of Jesus in 30 A.D. and the fall of Jerusalem in 70 A.D. in the war with Rome,

---

*Judas had committed suicide, presumably because of his betrayal of Jesus.

are Paul's Epistles and the Acts of the Apostles by Luke. Neither is a strictly historical document, both being written to shore up sagging faith and to boost declining morale.

In Jerusalem the apostles founded what became known as the Apostolic Church. The name conjures up the image of a beautiful building like the present Church of the Holy Sepulchre in Jerusalem. Alas, such was not the case. The Apostolic Church, founded forty days after the death of Jesus, consisted of an upper room in a nondescript building in the Zion section of Jerusalem, which was obliterated in the Rome–Jerusalem war.

It was a church in name only; in reality it was an "apostolic community" of some hundred and twenty souls, which multiplied within a decade to eight thousand. If there had been a Gallup poll taken in the Roman Empire in the year 31 A.D. asking: "Do you think that the Christian Church will be the ruler of this empire in three hundred years?" 99.9 percent would have answered "No."

For the first three decades, members of this Jewish "Jesus sect," known as the Nazarenes, were almost all Orthodox Jews, and their Christianity differed less radically from Phariseeism than Catholicism does today from Protestantism.

In his wry manner, Edward Gibbon has summed up the forty-year history of the Apostolic Church in one sentence, which pleases neither Christian nor Jew but brings a smile to the face of the agnostic, "The first fifteen bishops of Jerusalem," he wrote, "were all circumcised Jews; and the congregation over which they presided united the Laws of Moses with the doctrine of Christ."★

★Gibbon, *The Decline and Fall of the Roman Empire.*

We must remember that the early Apostolic Church did not possess the Epistles of Paul or the four Gospels, as they had not yet been written. The "Christianity" of the eleven disciples of Jesus, therefore, consisted of what they remembered of him and his sayings, of their ordeals and tribulations with him, and of legends and beliefs of their times, augmented and embellished by hope and need.

The Apostolic Church had no concept of a "resurrected Christ." He was viewed not as a divine being but as the "anointed one," the rightful King of Israel, who would return one day to help liberate that land from the giant oppressor of the world, the Roman Empire.

The Nazarenes remained as devoted to the Jewish Law as Jesus had been. They circumcised their male children, observed all dietary laws, and admitted to their ranks Sadducees and Pharisees, priests and scribes, provided they acknowledged that Jesus was the messiah. This in itself presented no problem to the Pharisees, who regarded "rising from the dead" as a Jewish phenomenon. For proof they cited the three accounts of "rising from the dead" in the Old Testament.* Thus, the only difference between the Nazarenes and the Pharisees was that the former believed their messiah *had arrived*, and the latter were waiting for their messiah *to arrive*. As for the Sadducees, they did not care either way, for they believed in no messianic doctrine.

Peter was the head of the Apostolic Church for the first two decades (30 to 50 A.D.). Like Jesus, Peter was circumcised, kept a kosher home, and observed all dietary laws until 50 A.D. in Antioch when he supped with Gentiles. But, unlike Jesus, he was married to a Jewish woman

---

*I Kings 17:22; II Kings 4:34, and 13:12.

named Perpetua. He seemed to have little organizational ability, and around 50 A.D. he lost his leadership in the Apostolic Church to James, the younger brother of Jesus, a newcomer to the Church.

James was a most unlikely candidate to head the Apostolic Church in view of his previously hostile attitude toward his older brother Jesus. James had been a doubting Thomas. Even after the crucifixion, James had not as yet converted to the new Christian sect. One day, however, according to Paul,★ Jesus appeared to his brother and won him over to the new faith. James in his own Epistle, however, makes no mention of such an encounter.★★ As for the rest of Jesus' family, his sisters had married local Jewish boys and stayed in Nazareth, but his mother and three other brothers—Simon, Joseph, and Judas—had moved to Jerusalem, where they had all joined the Apostolic Church.†

James's rise in the Apostolic Church was rapid. Known by the Jews as James the Just, he was an ardent Temple-goer who considered himself a hereditary high priest. He did not let his followers forget that his father Joseph was of royal ancestry; he had the ambition to continue that dynasty through himself. What James was working for was a reformation of the Jewish faith. According to Friedrich Gontard, he envisioned that through

---

★Corinthians 15:7. There is no other testimony to such an event.

★★The Epistle of James (written circa 45 A.D.) is the most controversial document in the New Testament, because its contents reflect Apostolic thinking, not Pauline. Luther, who based his Reformation on Paul, called James's Epistle "an Epistle of straw," because it did not preach salvation through the cross. The authorship of this Epistle is also in doubt.

†I Corinthians 3:7.

his brand of Jewish Christianity, Jerusalem would become
the true city of David.*

There was, however, a snake in the garden of the
Apostolic Church. It had no sacraments and no priesthood of its own to distinguish it from the Jewish religion.
The Nazarenes held readings from the Old Testament,
prayed the same prayers the Jews did, and observed the
same festivals. The Nazarenes were in danger of becoming absorbed back into the Judaism from which Jesus had
sprung. Into this tranquil but potentially dangerous scene
for Christianity stepped a young Pharisee Jew by the
name of Saul of Tarsus, later to be known by his Ro-
manized name Paul, destined to become the painter of
the sixth face of Jesus—the Christ.

When Paul (died 64 or 67 A.D.) entered the stage of
Christian history, he had a hard act to follow. The climax
had come and gone. Who could upstage a crucifixion?
Most heroes are vouchsafed only one grand entry into
history, but considering his handicap, one must not be-
grudge Paul the three tries history granted him. The first
was as a participant in the lynching of an apostle; the
second was an encounter with Jesus himself; and the third
was a quarrel with James, the brother of Jesus. The first
two entries, despite their inherent drama, fizzled; he made
it on the third, the drabbest of the three.

A minor fluke of history paved the way for Paul's
first entry on the Christian scene. The rule of the Apostolic Church had been smooth the first two years. Then
trouble started with the stoning of the apostle Stephen
(about 32 A.D.), the first Christian martyr. Stephen had
gone just a step too far in his zeal when he publicly pro-

*Gontard, *The Chair of Peter: A History of the Papacy*. Holt,
Rinehart, and Winston, 1964.

145

claimed that Temple attendance was a form of idolatry and that Jesus was the literal son of God who had replaced Mosaic Law. That did it. Even before the death sentence by the Sanhedrin had been announced, an enraged mob seized him and stoned him to death, without consulting the Romans.

This stoning party may have launched the career of "the real founder of Christianity" according to many theologians, for Paul was a member of that lynch mob. He also may well have been the one to cast the first stone in the execution of Stephen, for he had been the principal witness against him. It was this former Pharisee and chief executioner of the first Christian martyr who was destined to carry the creed from its cramped Jewish quarter in Jerusalem to the Roman Empire and shape it into a world force.

Did history smile when she capriciously chose Paul, the son of a tentmaker in Tarsus, Cilicia (now part of Turkey), to found the Church Peter had failed to establish?* If Paul had lived today, he might have ended up on a psychiatrist's couch. Throughout his life he was overwhelmed with an all-pervasive sense of guilt that pursued him with a relentless fury. He was given to recurrent attacks of malaria, had repeated hallucinations, and, some scholars believe, was subject to epileptic seizures. He was celibate and exhorted others to celibacy. Paul never mentioned his father or mother, and he was never baptized.

From early paintings, and from descriptions of him

---

*Even though the Vatican attributes the founding of the Church to Peter, history does not provide enough facts to support that view. Paul was its logical architect, and Peter got the credit.

in the New Testament, we have a rather repellent picture of Paul. Luke, who knew him personally, gives us a most unflattering portrait of him, almost that of a caricature of a ghetto Jew—a little man with a big, bald head, bushy eyebrows, blind in one eye, with crooked legs and a big nose. Ernest Renan characterized him as "the ugly little Jew." The German philosopher Friedrich Nietzsche summed up Paul in terms usually reserved for Jews by anti-Semites. Paul, said this syphilitic prototype of the Nazi Superman, was a man "whose superstition was equaled by his cunning." To Martin Luther, he was a "rock of strength."

Intellectually, however, Paul was a blend of his times—a Jew by birth, a Roman by citizenship, and a product of Greek culture. His education was eclectic—Roman law, Greek philosophy, and Jewish Oral Law. He journeyed to Jerusalem to study under the renowned Rabbi Gamaliel at about the same time Jesus came to Jerusalem to preach, but the two never met. A devout and observing Jew, "a Pharisee of Pharisees," as he styled himself, Paul could have become a famed Talmudist; instead history made him a Christian saint. But whereas Jesus was a messiah-intoxicated Jew who died a Jew, Paul became a Christ-intoxicated Jew who died a Christian.

Four years went by after the incident at Stephen's Gate (as the place where Stephen was stoned, near one of the gates in Old Jerusalem, is now called) and nothing happened. Had Paul been brooding over his part in the stoning? We do not know, but the stage was set for his second entry into Christian history, one that many psychologists feel may have been triggered by such a guilt motif.

After the incident with Stephen, Paul had become a

fanatic persecutor of Christians, not only locally, but internationally. According to Acts,* the high priest in Jerusalem had given Paul carte-blanche letters to go to Damascus to arrest any and all Christians he could find and bring them back as prisoners for trial in Jerusalem.

This entire story in Acts does not make historical sense. There is no evidence that the Sanhedrin had an international program of persecuting Christians. Not even Rome had such a program in 36 A.D. The high priest had no authority to issue carte-blanche orders for the arrest of anyone in Jerusalem, still less for anyone in Damascus, which was not under Jewish rule. Besides, why send someone to Damascus to arrest Christians when they were, according to Luke, right there in the Jerusalem Temple every day praying with the rest of the worshipers? The story defies logic, but it is a dramatic introduction to what was to happen next.

It was on this mission on the road to Damascus that Paul had his famous encounter with his vision of Jesus. "Why dost thou persecute me?" Jesus asked him. Paul was blinded physically by this vision and had to be led helpless to Damascus. Here a Nazarene Jew named Ananias cured Paul's blindness and converted him to the Nazarene sect, not by baptizing but by laying hands upon him.

Did Jesus actually manifest himself to Paul? We could equally well ask, did God actually manifest Himself to Abraham? From a historical viewpoint it makes little difference whether these were real encounters or hallucinations. The fact remains that just as Abraham's encounter with God played a dominant role in the subsequent four thousand years of Jewish history, so Paul's encounter with Jesus has had an equally dominant part

---

*Acts 2:1–2.

in the subsequent two thousand years of Christian history. This is the reality we must deal with, for it is the reality of faith that created history.

Paul's second entry into history also failed, however. He vanished for another eleven years, until a Nazarene disciple named Barnabas asked Paul to accompany him on a missionary journey. Curiously enough, Paul and Barnabas became known among the pagan Greeks as Zeus and Hermes—father and son.

It was on this journey that the future "Christianity" shaped itself in Paul's mind. He made three decisions. His first, since Jews had not stampeded to the Nazarene sect, was to take the faith to the pagans. To make it easier for the Gentiles to join his new religion, he made a second decision, that of abandoning circumcision and dietary laws. His third decision was to substitute Jesus "the Flesh" for the Torah, "the Word." This concept was the most crucial, for it caused the final and unalterable break between Judaism (the "Father religion") and Christianity (the "son religion").

When Paul returned from this missionary journey (50 A.D.), he headed for Jerusalem to confront James with his resolves. The Apostolic Church now faced a crisis. The meeting between James and Paul was stormy. In the end a compromise was reached. The decision was made to divide the missionary territory—Paul got the Gentiles and James got the Jews. Or, as the New Testament expresses it, James became the apostle of the circumcised and Paul the apostle of the uncircumcised. With this "third entry" into Christian history, Paul became the dominant personality and James the recessive. It is doubtful whether James ever understood the significance of Paul's views, which changed his brother Jesus from a Jewish messiah-rabbi into the Christ.

In the entire panoply of colorful characters inhabiting the New Testament, none has a sense of humor except Paul. One famed outburst occurred in his argument with the Galatians concerning circumcision. "Look, if we are in union with Christ Jesus," says Paul, "circumcision makes no difference at all, nor the want of it." Then he added wryly, "And as for these circumcision agitators, they might as well go the entire way and cut the whole thing off." *The New English Bible* states it a little more delicately: "As for these agitators, they had better go the whole way and make eunuchs of themselves."★

There are two theological arguments about Paul. One is that he "invented Christianity" and perverted the true religion of Jesus, a view trenchantly expressed by Nietzsche, the apostle of the German superman, before he died in an insane asylum:

> Paul embodies the very opposite type to that of Jesus. . . . Paul is a genius of hatred, in his vision of hate, in the ruthless logic of hate. What has this nefarious evangelist not sacrificed to his hatred? He crucified his savior on the cross . . . he made him into a god who died for our sins . . . resurrection after death—all these are falsifications of true Christianity, for which that morbid crank must be made responsible.

On the other hand, there is the view that does not believe all truth reposes in Nietzsche. This position holds that after Jesus, Paul was the first pure Christian, that though he did not invent Christianity or pervert it, he rescued it from extinction.

★Galatians 5:12.

After his break with the Apostolic Church, Paul set out on his next two now-famous missionary journeys, but without Barnabas with whom he also had had a quarrel. This time he had two other male companions, Silas and Timothy, the latter a gentle, passive companion whom Paul personally circumcised before he abolished circumcision as an entry requirement into Christianity. It was also during these journeys, between 50 and 62 A.D., that Paul wrote most of his famed Epistles (Letters), which, along with the Gospels, form the heart of the New Testament. They are the earliest Christian writings.

As Paul journeyed throughout the Roman Empire, he used synagogues as pulpits for his missionary sermons, for the synagogue was a most tolerant institution, permitting many divergent views. Paul, however, was not equally tolerant. In those same synagogues he threatened that "If any man preach any other Gospel unto you than you have received from me let him be accursed."

More than anything, Paul craved to receive the title of Apostle, but twice the Apostolic Church rebuked him by not granting it to him. In the end Paul conferred the apostolic title on himself, claiming he received it from Jesus.

It was not history that impressed the sixth face on Jesus but Paul. His entire life, from the revelation on the road to Damascus to his death in Rome, was a quest for a total identification with Jesus, in body and spirit, in soul and mind. As he himself described it, his encounter with Jesus was an ecstatic identification with him. Jesus, he said, appeared not *to* him but *in* him.

After the confrontation with James, subsequent events in the life of Paul became a syndromic recapitulation of the events in the life of Jesus. Jesus had felt compelled to go to Jerusalem to be first arrested by the priests and then tried and put to death by the Romans. Paul's life now became a compulsive replica of the Jesus model.

On his return from his third missionary journey, Paul headed for Jerusalem, where he went out of his way deliberately to defile the Temple by taking an uncircumcised Gentile into the inner sanctum, which he knew was an offense punishable by death. He was arrested by the priests and held for trial.

If there was a compulsive recapitulation of the life of Jesus in the life of Paul, then the Pauline script should call for a trial and execution by the Romans, not the Jews. That is precisely what happened. Paul compelled the Jews to send him to Rome for a trial by invoking his Roman citizenship, which granted him that privilege.

The psychodrama continued. As the ship taking Paul to Rome almost sank in a storm, Paul related that an angel appeared to him saying, "Fear not. You must be brought before Caesar." Paul stated he was saved from the storm for the specific purpose of appearing for punishment before Caesar. But fate would not yet cooperate. He was set free by the Romans because there were no witnesses against him.

However, Paul compelled fate to grant him the expiatory death he sought. Compulsively he returned to Rome (after a voyage to Spain, some scholars aver), despite warnings against doing so. He was arrested and this time sentenced to death. But because a Roman citizen could not be crucified, he was beheaded.* The exact year is not known.

Paul succeeded in turning an "inglorious crucifixion

---

*This compulsion of Paul to identify his life with that of Jesus compels us to consider the remarkable parallelism between the lives of Paul, Jesus, and the Teacher of Righteousness.

into a glorious resurrection." In the words of Johannes
Lehman: "He made a victorious Christ out of a failed
Jewish messiah . . . the son of God out of the son of
man."* In characteristic fashion, Paul himself summed it
up better than any paraphrase could. "Jews demand signs
and Greeks seek wisdom, but we preach Christ crucified. . . . If Christ has not been raised, then our preaching
has been in vain and your faith in vain." Paul was the
first to state Christ was resurrected and walked on earth.
With that thought, Christianity was born. The word
"Christian" was coined by Paul (around 50 A.D.) when
he used it to describe his disciples in Antioch.**

Jesus and Paul, each in his own way, gave impetus
to Christianity as a world movement. But, many scholars
feel, it was Paul who shaped and marketed it. It was Paul
who made the "risen Christ" central to Christianity. Paul
preached a doctrine perhaps unknown to the first Apostolic Nazarenes—salvation through the cross. In this
sense, Paul's portrayal of Jesus as "the Christ" is the sixth
face of Jesus.

There remains but one more face to explore in our
quest for the historical Jesus before we can synthesize all
seven into one synoptic view. We will now have to abandon the canonical Gospels for an examination of the
Gnostic Gospels, which give a counterview—the seventh
face of Jesus.

---

*Rabbi J.
**The word "Christianity" does not appear even once in the
entire New Testament, and the word "Christian" appears but
three times—twice in Acts (11:26, 26:28) and once in Peter
(4:16).

Chapter 10

Christian Gnostics and Their Scandalizing Gospels

T he credulity of the reader may already have been strained by the account of how a teenage Arab black-marketeer discovered the Dead Sea Scrolls, which linked a sect of Jews to a practice of Christianity a century before the birth of Jesus. Now that credulity will have to be stretched further with an account of how an illiterate Egyptian peasant discovered the Gnostic Gospels, which link a sect of early Christians to the practice of libertin-ism* a century after the death of Jesus.

The discovery of the Gnostic Gospels reads like a modern story of intrigue beginning in the sands of Egypt, then settling on the international black markets of Cairo and New York. The tale begins in the spring of 1945, in a sand-soaked corner of the world, a small mud-hut ham-

---

*From "libertine," a person who is unrestrained by morality, leading a dissolute life.

let named Nag Hammadi in Upper Egypt, where a peasant named Muhammed and his two brothers saddled their camels to set out in search of a load of fertilizer. Digging around a boulder, Muhammed's spade hit a red earthenware jar, three feet high. The hope of finding gold overcame his fear of releasing an evil spirit; he smashed the jar, which contained what later proved to be thirteen codices (papyrus manuscripts bound in leather) comprising fifty-three Gnostic Gospels. Disgusted with his priceless find, Muhammed dumped the codices on a pile of straw next to the fireplace in his home. His mother, may she rest in peace, burned one of the fifty-three gospels along with some straw for kindling.

A few days after the discovery, Muhammed and his brothers killed a man they suspected of having slain their father. The brothers "hacked off his limbs, ripped out his heart, and ate it," according to the official report, as the ultimate act of blood revenge. Fearing a police search, Muhammed asked a mullah—an Islamic priest—to hold the manuscripts for him. A local teacher stole one and sold it to an antiquities dealer on the Cairo black market. The Egyptian authorities, hearing of the sale, traced the stolen codices to the priest, but found only eleven, not twelve codices in his possession. Someone else had managed to steal another codex★ and smuggle it out of Egypt. It surfaced on the New York antiquities market in 1955.

After years of haggling and litigation, twelve of the thirteen codices are now housed in the Coptic Museum in Cairo. By 1977, all had been translated into English and published. But it was the thirteenth codex, smuggled out of Egypt, that centered world attention on the discovery. There is little doubt that had these gospels come

---

★A codex contained three to five gospels.

to light in the Middle Ages they would have been burned along with the discoverers. In those days the codices would have been viewed as subversive and heretical. Today, they are archaeological gems.

Among the most important of these fifty-two remaining texts are the *Gospel of Thomas*, the *Gospel of Philip*, *Gospel to the Hebrews*, *Secret Book of James*, *The Apocalypse of Paul*, and *The Apocalypse of Peter*. Whereas the Dead Sea Scrolls described the Jewish world out of which Christianity had arisen, these Gnostic Gospels delineated the heretic beliefs that almost tore Christianity apart in the first four centuries of its life.

The scholarly world was in an uproar. The authenticity of these codices was undisputed. Though the gospels contained were dated around 350–450 A.D., scholars knew the original texts dated back to as early as 120 to 150 A.D., because Church Fathers from the second century had referred to many of them in their writings. Everyone had assumed that all Gnostic gospels had long since been destroyed, and some theologians wish they had been. The claim in these texts that Jesus had been romantically linked with Mary Magdalene, and had perhaps even been married to her, was but a prelude to other, more scandalous revelations.

But how did these Gnostic Gospels find their way into a three-foot red earthenware jar, buried near a huge stone in a field of fertilizer outside Nag Hammadi in Upper Egypt? The answer is simple. They were hidden in that jar and buried in that field around 500 A.D. by a Coptic* Christian monk, probably from the nearby monastery of Saint Pachomius, because he did not want to be put to

---

*The Copts are Christian Egyptians, a branch of the Eastern Orthodox Church. The Copts maintain that their Church in Alexandria was founded by Saint Mark himself.

death for possessing them. By the fifth century A.D., the Gnostic Gospels had become heretical documents in the eyes of the then-dominant Catholic Church. The persecuted had become the persecutors.

The shift in power from the pagans to the Christians was achieved in four swift strokes. With the Edict of Milan (313), Rome reversed its policy of persecuting the Christians. In 367, Athanasius, Bishop of Alexandria, commanded the destruction of all gospels, except the four authorized in the New Testament. In 380, Emperor Theodosius established Christianity as the state religion of the Roman Empire and, with his Edict in 394, closed all pagan temples, ending among other things the Olympic Games. The final stroke came in 416, when it was decreed that non-Christians—including pagans, Zoroastrians, Jews, and Gnostic Christians—would be forbidden to hold public office and that possession of all nonauthorized gospels would be a crime punishable by death. Thus, within a century, those who had once been fed to the lions now figuratively threw others to them.

And thus it came about that in the fifth century a monk in Upper Egypt, in possession of fifty-three Gnostic gospels bound in thirteen codices, was in fear of his life. He had to get rid of these incriminating documents. As he could not bring himself to destroy these, to him, sacred texts, he chose the Jewish way out. He buried them in the ground in a jar so nature would do the job for him and thus absolve him from the heinous deed of desecrating divine revelation. Nature, however, did not cooperate. One-and-a-half millennia later, the earth cast forth the documents that had been entrusted to it.

But who were the Gnostics?

The Gnostics could be described as a dropout sect of Christian hippies, and their faith could be viewed as a left-wing, sex-oriented, swinging religion that flourished on the peripheries of paganism, Christianity, and Judaism. Toward the end of the second century, this offbeat movement threatened to become the dominant Christian religion.

What gave the Gnostics such impetus in their quest for dominance was that they were not Johnny-come-lately Christians. Like the first twelve disciples of Jesus, the first Christian Gnostics were also Jews who had been among the first followers of Jesus. They were there at the Golden Gate to greet him as he rode into Jerusalem on the colt of an ass, welcoming him with shouts of "Hosanna, son of David." They were there that Good Friday at Golgotha when Jesus was crucified. They were there in Jerusalem when the Apostolic Church opened its doors. However, the Gnostics viewed the same phenomena differently than Mark, Matthew, Luke, and John did a generation or two later.

By the second century, the Gnostics, like the "orthodox Christians," were no longer former Jews but former pagans converted to Christianity. Feeling the need for books giving their own views of Jesus, the Gnostics began to write gospels at about the same time John composed his—around 110–40 A.D. Just about every tenet in the Four Gospels was disputed by the Gnostics, and this placed them on a collision course with the "orthodox" or Pauline Christians.

The main story line in the Gnostic Gospels follows that of the evangelists. Jesus is baptized; he speaks in parables; he heals, performs miracles, gathers his disciples, gets in trouble with priests and Pharisees, is arrested, is tried by Pilate, and is crucified.

But here the similarities end. The Nag Hammadi texts hold that Jesus was not born of a virgin mother but came into the world in the ordinary nonvirgin way; that he had a twin brother named Judas Thomas; that Jesus viewed Peter as a numbskull; that his relations with Mary Magdalene were not ascetic but erotic. To quote from the Gnostic *Gospel of Philip*:

> . . . the companion of the [Savior is] Mary Magdalene. [But Christ loved] her more than [all] the disciples, and used to kiss her [often] on her [mouth]. The rest of [the disciples were offended]. . . . They said to him "why do you love her more than all of us"? The Savior answered, and said to them, "Why do I not love you as [I love] her."*

The Gnostics denied the apostolic succession through Peter, claiming it was through Mary Magdalene, and ranked her as the chief apostle. Also, according to the *Gospel of Philip*, Jesus was married to her. Elaine Pagels** suggests that there are strong indications in the Nag Hammadi texts that the Gnostic trinity was composed of the Father, the son, and the mother as the third partner, not the Holy Ghost.

The most shocking aspect of these Nag Hammadi texts is the Gnostic belief that Jesus was not flesh and blood, but a spiritual being, immune to death. Thus he did not die on the cross, but was only perceived to have died. The crucifixion, aver the Gnostics, was only a spiritual event in the minds of his followers.

Is there corroboration for this view in the Gospels?

---

*Elaine Pagels, *The Gnostic Gospels*. Random House, New York, 1979.
**Ibid.

Luke reports that Jesus appeared to his disciples, after his crucifixion, in another, not his earthly form. When Jesus met two of his disciples on the road to Emmaus, says Luke, they did not recognize him until he sat down to dinner with them, after which he just vanished.

Other Gnostic texts go further and relate that it was not Jesus who was crucified but Simon of Cyrene. Thus the *Second Treatise of the Great Seth* relates that Jesus told Peter, "It was another who drank the gall and vinegar; it was not I. . . . It was another, Simon [of Cyrene] who bore the cross on his shoulders. It was another upon whom they placed the crown of thorns. . . ."★

The Gnostics had no formal priesthood and used a lottery system to determine who should hold priestly posts. Women could both be priests and serve the Eucharist meal. To add insult to injury, several Gnostic texts held the peculiar doctrine that God was an ignoramus who had an exaggerated opinion of his own importance, and who now and then had to be reproved by a superior, unspecified deity—a woman.

Some Gnostic Gospels provide two other pejorative comments about Jesus. One is to say that Jesus was a thaumaturgist, that is, a sorcerer and magician. The second is to picture Jesus as a libertine, the leader of an esoteric sex cult. Some also aver that Jesus studied magic in Egypt, that it was as a magician and exorcist that he made the deepest impression upon his contemporaries, and that "this remained the principal character of his veneration by the Christian Church for years to come."★★

We must remember, say scholars holding to this

★Elaine Pagels, *The Gnostic Gospels*.
★★ *The Beginnings of the Gospels*, by C. F. Evans, as quoted in Michael Grant, *Jesus, An Historian's View of the Gospels*. Charles Scribner's Sons, New York 1977.

school of thought, that at the time Jesus lived, words had magic and

> healing was secured by touching the healer or his gar-
> ments . . . where saliva is applied to tongue and eyes,
> where the touch or grasp of the healer's hand . . .
> effects immediate cure. . . .★

The Gospel of Mark states Jesus did precisely this. According to Mark, Jesus cured a deaf mute by putting his finger in the ear of the patient, spitting, touching his tongue, and pronouncing the magic word *Eph'phatha*.★★ By laying his hands on a blind man, says Mark, and spitting in the blind man's eyes, Jesus cured him.† And he raised the daughter of Jairus from the dead with the magic phrase *talitha cumi*, and by touching her hand.‡

The pernicious influence of these libertine Gnostics was already felt in the time of Paul, for we find denunciation of their practices in his Epistles. In Galatians,†† Paul warned, "You were called to freedom, brethren—only do not use your freedom for the flesh."

In Philippians,‡‡ he stated that there were many going about as Christians who were enemies of the cross. "Their end," warned Paul, "is destruction, their god is the belly, and they glory in their shame." And in Ephesians††† he

---

★G. Vermes, *Jesus the Jew*.
★★Mark 7:33.
†Mark 8:23.
‡Mark 5:41.
††Galatians 5:13.
‡‡Philippians 3:18.
†††Ephesians 5:1–20.

launched a campaign against practices by Christians "that are shameful to mention the things they do in secret."

There is only one point on which all contending parties—Jesus, Jews, Romans, evangelists, Gnostics, and scholars—agree, and that is that Jesus was crucified on the orders of Pontius Pilate. All disagree, however, on the reason. According to Jesus himself, it was in fulfillment of his prediction. According to the evangelists, it was the Jews who conspired against Jesus. According to the Jews and Romans, it was because Jesus rebelled against Rome. With the discovery of the Gnostic Gospels, a new reason surfaced, that Jesus was executed by the Romans for his libertinism.

Do the Gospels and history support these Gnostic views?

Throughout the synoptic Gospels, the evangelists record that Jesus and his followers were often accused of being wine-imbibers, gluttons, associates of tax collectors, whores, thieves, and an exotic assortment of other sinners. Gnostic versions of Christian beliefs and rites could lead one to believe that the Roman historians who stressed the libertine and licentious nature of the early Christians might be accurate. Thus, for instance, the aristocratic Roman historian Tacitus (55–117?), to explain why Nero selected the Christians as suspects in setting fire to Rome and why he punished them with the utmost refinements of cruelty, wrote in his *Annals* that there was

a class of persons hated for their vices, whom the people called Christians. Christus, the founder of the name, had undergone the death penalty in the reign of Tiberius, by sentence of the procurator Pontius Pilate, and the pernicious superstition was checked for the moment, only to break out once more in Judea, the home of the disease, but also in the capital itself, where everything horrible or shameful in the world gathers and becomes fashionable.

Tacitus went on to state that the Christians were really persecuted, not for being suspected of setting fire to Rome, but for their presumed hatred of the human race. The Christians were identified with their leader "Christus," whom the Romans thought of as a magician and a libertine who was executed for treason.

The Gnostic counterview of Jesus and Christianity reminds one of Andersen's fairy tale *The Snow Queen*, where Satan crafted a mirror in which all values are reflected in a distorted fashion. One day, a coven of devils, transporting the mirror from one place to another, dropped it. The mirror shattered into a million fragments, some the size of specks of dust, each speck having the magic of the entire mirror. Thousands upon thousands of these specks became lodged in the eyes of the people, who then perceived everything in a perverse fashion—the true as false and the false as true, the beautiful as ugly and the ugly as beautiful.

And thus it was with the Gnostic Gospels. Everything in the New Testament was interpreted by them in reverse. The sacred was made profane and the profane sacred. Rites of redemption were presented as orgiastic happenings; God became evil and the serpent wise.

Every religion, no matter how noble its intent, has its counterpart in "gnostics" who see religion in their own image rather than in the image its founder conceived. They are there, like the specks from Satan's mirror, to mock and deceive. Judaism, too, has not been immune from such a "gnostic spell." In the eighteenth century, Judaism was swept into a "Jewish gnostic" religious sex cult known as Frankism, which at one point embraced a sizable segment of Europe's Jews. An Asian, unfamiliar with either the Old Testament or Jewish history, would judge, based on the freak Frankist movement, that Judaism was a religion that included group sex, incest, homosexuality, and lesbianism.

To attribute the rites practiced by the Frankists as authentic Judaism because the Frankists were Jews, is just as absurd as to attribute to authentic Christianity the vices practiced by the Gnostics. Gnosticism eventually died out in the fifth century, not under the impact of Christian and Jewish bans, but because in the long run the moral teachings of the Old and New Testaments proved stronger than group sex and blasphemy.

In addition to the moral suasion, there was a practical reason why the Church prevailed. Gnosticism atrophied and died because of its own internal weakness. Each Gnostic doing his or her thing did not promote stability. Choosing priests and bishops by lot rather than on merit or faith could not produce a lasting and devoted hierarchy or a stable, organized Church. Whatever strength had motivated Gnosticism in the beginning was weakened and diluted by sex-oriented mysticism, until the movement collapsed.

Throughout the history of both Judaism and Christianity, heretical sects have arisen to challenge the central core of the beliefs of each. But in every challenge, history has had the good judgment to select the Judaism of Moses and the Christianity of Jesus as victors over the dissenters.

Thus, the seventh face of Jesus—as a Gnostic—must be rejected as unhistorical.

Until now, each aspect of Jesus has been seen through a kaleidoscope in which the total picture has been fragmented into scholarly abstractions. We can now attempt to synthesize these seven faces of Jesus into one synoptic view in the hopes that one historical Jesus might emerge.

PART THREE

The Aftermath

Chapter 11

The Troika of Moses, Jesus, and Paul

We have explored the seven faces of Jesus that theologians and secular scholars have unveiled, but rejected the seventh, the Gnostic, as unhistorical. Which then of the remaining six portrays the real Jesus?

To restate the questions we asked in the first chapter: Is Jesus the Christian messiah, the literal son of God as averred by the devout? Is he a Jewish messiah, the son of man, stripped of his Jewish garments and robed in Christian vestments posthumously? Is he a Zealot who tried to wrest the throne of David from the Roman oppressors by force? Is he the "sublime strategist" who engineered his own messiahship because he sincerely believed he was the messiah? Is he an Essene, a member of an obscure Jewish religious sect that practiced a form of Christianity a century before his birth? Is he the Christ, a divine mystique, through whose flesh and blood man may find salvation, as preached by Paul?

Which of these six portraits depicts the historical Jesus? Is he any one of them, none of them, some of them, or, perhaps, a combination of all?

This multifaceted presentation of Jesus is reminiscent of the defense of an art dealer accused of having returned an antique vase in a broken condition. The art dealer pleaded that first he had never borrowed the vase, second, it was broken when he borrowed it, and that third, it was in perfect condition when he returned it. Has this presentation, in like manner, pleaded that if Jesus was not a Zealot he must have been a "messianic plotter," or if he did not engineer his own messiahship, then he must have been an Essene? Or if these arguments fail, then—falling back on other lines of defense—that Jesus perhaps was nothing but a minor Jewish prophet, or an idea spun in Paul's mind?

We have seen, in each chapter, an otherwise enigmatic segment in the life of Jesus fall into place like a piece in a perplexing puzzle the moment it was dropped into the right slot. Thus, the Transfiguration fits perfectly into the concept of Jesus as the son of God. The enigma of the two trials resolves itself when placed in the slot of Jesus as a Jew; the riddle of Barabbas is unraveled only when Jesus is viewed as a Zealot; Judas and Pilate become comprehensible in historical terms the instant they are made part of a prophetic scenario.

Could it be that there are elements of all these in the life of Jesus? Can these diverse elements be blended into one portrait consistent both with the Gospel accounts and with history? They can, say many historians.

Jesus—the script of these synoptic historians goes—born of Jewish parents in Nazareth, spent his early life in

Egypt, at that time the center of learning for the science of performing miracles and effecting wonder cures. Returning to Judea in his early youth, he joined the Essene community around Qumran, becoming imbued with the Essene ideas of asceticism, resurrection, and immortality. About the age of thirty, he became convinced he was the messiah and decided to test that conviction against the blueprint of the prophets. If he accomplished everything the prophets had said the messiah would have to fulfill —such fulfillment would then prove he was the messiah.

Jesus left the Essene monastery. John the Baptist, an Essene making a path for the Lord in the wilderness, recognized in Jesus the awaited messiah and baptized (anointed) him, thus fulfilling the first prophecy.

Jesus now repaired to the wilderness for forty days, where he overcame the doubts assailing him. Convinced of the rightness of his cause, he decided to put his convictions into action. He joined the outlaw Zealots in order to fulfill the prophecy that the messiah had to be a transgressor.

But first his vision of the kingdom of God would have to be made acceptable to the people. He embarked on his messianic career as a wonder healer and performer of miracles, two prerequisites also stipulated by the prophets for an aspirant to the messianic crown. He built his Zealot organization through his twelve disciples, most of them trusted Galileeans.

After a year, Jesus was ready.* Having briefed his disciples as to his identity and destiny, he entered Jerusalem on Palm Sunday a triumphant hero. He wrested the Temple from the Romans, held it for an unknown period of time, then surrendered himself to them after

---

*Three years, according to John.

finessing the Jews into arresting him, again in order to fulfill prescribed prophecies. At this point, his Zealot disciples, confused and disappointed by this course of events, deserted him.

A hearing was held before the Sanhedrin. The high priest tried to persuade Jesus to plead innocent to all charges of sedition against him by the Romans, but to no avail. Jesus was not deterred because he had predicted his death by crucifixion, which would be attained only after a Roman trial. The high priest rent his clothes in despair according to Jewish custom, and Jesus had to be delivered to the Romans on orders of Pilate.

Accused of aspiring to be King of the Jews, Jesus pleaded what today is known as nolo contendere—a no-contest defense. Pilate sentenced him to death by crucifixion for high treason.

Taken off the cross by Joseph of Arimathea, Jesus was interred in a tomb in Joseph's private garden.

Thus far this synoptic view of history and faith fits all four Gospel accounts in their essential points. But what happened next? What happened after Mary went to the tomb of Jesus to find the stone rolled away from the entrance and the body of Jesus gone? Had he been dead or alive when taken off the cross? Had he risen, or been spirited away?

Here the quest for the historical Jesus must end. There are no answers, only speculation. But we do have our six faces of Jesus and the possibility that they are all different aspects of one enigmatic individual.

This one individual, this Jew Jesus, conquered history. So powerful was Jesus' appeal to the pagans of the Roman Empire that within fifty years of his death, pagan converts to Christianity outnumbered the Jewish ones. Within a century, Christianity was no longer regarded as a Jewish sect by the Romans but seen as a distinct and separate religion of no specific nationality. Paul had taken a handful of dispirited disciples of Jesus and transformed them into a Church militant that, within three centuries after the death of Paul, became the inheritor of the Roman Empire.

Paul's perception of Jesus was eventually imposed by the Church upon all Christendom. It became the new, authenticated Christianity, a faith perhaps alien to Peter and James. Religion, like history, is written by the victors.

Though Paul became an apostle to the Gentiles and abolished Mosaic law, he nevertheless held that Christianity and the Old Testament were indissoluble. So pervasive was Paul's influence that when at the end of the third century the New Testament was canonized, it was combined with the Old Testament into one Holy Scripture. Thus, in spite of the Trinity, Jewish monotheism was maintained within Christianity.

Three consequences flowed from this merger: Christianity was saved from being immersed in paganism; the spirit of Judaism was preserved in the Christian body; and the foundation was laid for a future Judeo-Christian civilization.

It was the combined impact of the Decalogue of Moses and the Beatitudes of Jesus that saved Christianity from degenerating into paganism after having ingested so many millions of pagan converts in so short a time. Rome's paganism had no spiritual message to give its people, only poverty for the masses and unsatisfying luxuries for the rich. With the combined Old and New Testaments, the Church held out hope for the downtrodden masses. All souls were given equal status.

To prevent the new Christian religion from becoming engulfed by a multitude of competing pagan creeds, the Church maintained selected Jewish institutions as a fence around its faith, though carefully giving them Christian names. The Temple in Jerusalem became the Vatican in Rome; the synagogue became the church; the rabbis became priests; the *tzitzes*, the fringed ritual garment worn by Jews and Jesus, became the scapular of the monks; Jewish liturgical music became the Gregorian chant. Thus a Jewish spirit pervaded the Church, not a pagan one.

The third, and most important, consequence was the political role the Church played in advancing Judeo-Christian civilization. With his conversion, Constantine's banner became the cross, Rome was baptized, Pope Gregory the Great (590–604) set out to plant the Gospels in the heartland of pagan Europe, and by the thirteenth century, the Latins and Nordics were united into one faith. While Christianity's salvation doctrine held the immediate attraction, it was the moral and ethical precepts of the Old Testament that gave the conquering Church her long-range values. In that sense, the Christians were the conquering arm of Judaism, and Christianity a stepping-stone by which the former pagans of Europe crossed over into Judaic precepts.

The reassessments of twentieth-century scholars have vitiated the terrifying effects of the German Protestant debunkers of Jesus and Christianity, restored the theological Jesus to his rightful place in history, and shown that looking historically at Jesus is not an offense to religion as Albert Schweitzer had warned but a help to an understanding of Jesus—not only for those who view him as the son of God, but also for those who do not.

Whichever view one accepts—Jesus as the son of

God, as the son of man, as a prophet, or as a Hebrew sage—one thing remains indisputable: Jesus is the central personality in a remarkable trinity—Moses, Jesus, and Paul—a trinity that gave birth to Western Civilization.

This is no mean achievement for three Jews.

BIBLIOGRAPHY

BIBLES

As text reference, I have used mainly four basic Bibles.

Towering over all Bible translations is the *King James Version*, still unsurpassed in sheer beauty and narrative power, which often captures the cadence and impact of the original Hebrew. Though the translation may not be as accurate as some scholars might wish, nevertheless the magnificence of its prose makes up for its occasional minor errors.

The *Oxford Annotated Bible*, Revised Standard Version, retains much of the sweep of the King James translation, though it has dropped many archaic words and phrases. The footnotes are excellent—often amazingly bold, though sometimes amazingly orthodox.

There are many "modern" translations that, to their literary detriment, have abandoned the King James blueprint. One happy exception is *The New English Bible* (The New Testament was published first in 1961 and the Old in 1970), cosponsored by the Oxford and Cambridge University Presses under the aegis of the General Assembly of the Church of Scotland. After the first shock wears off, it makes fascinating reading.

The *Simon and Schuster Bible, Designed to be Read as Living Literature*, is recommended for non-Bible readers. The translation is the King James version, but all "begats" and chronologies have been eliminated. It is set in eye-pleasing fourteen-point Goudy, and the sentences are not numbered.

In 1917, the Jewish Publication Society of America published what many consider the best Anglo-Jewish translation of the Old Testament (The Holy Scriptures, Philadelphia, The Jewish Publication Society, 1955) based on the Hebrew Masoretic (authoritative) text. While this translation hews mainly to that of the King James version, it is a rather stodgy work, though its scholarship is more reliable. It is regrettable that this volume has no footnotes. However, it has parallel columns of the Hebrew and English texts, which is helpful to those who understand Hebrew but are not fluent enough to follow the narrative without a parallel English translation.

GENERAL REFERENCE

Blair, Edward P. *Abingdon Bible Handbook.* Abingdon Press, Nashville, 1975. A superb guidebook through the maze of dates and ideas in the two Testaments.

Cruden, Alexander. *Cruden's Unabridged Concordance.* Grand Rapids, Michigan, Baker Book House, 1963. The amazing work of an eighteenth-century Scot who, after confinement for several years in an insane asylum as a result of an unrequited love for a woman who spurned him for a love affair with one of her brothers, began counting and indexing every word in the Old and New Testaments, so that today anyone can become an instant authority on who said what and where in the Bible by merely using his Concordance in the prescribed manner.

Delaney, John J. *Dictionary of Saints.* New York, Doubleday & Company, 1980. Tells you all you might reasonably want to know about saints, including the information that Saint Joseph, husband of Mary (sainted without a prior conversion to Christianity) is the saint of working men and of social justice.

Eiselen, Frederick Carl. *The Abingdon Bible Commentary*. New York, Abingdon Press, 1929. A remarkable work of compressed scholarship, objectivity, and lucidity; perhaps the best one-volume Bible commentary for the layperson.

Hastings, James, ed. *Encyclopedia of Religion and Ethics*. New York, Scribner's, 1951.

Miller, Madeleine S. and Miller, J. Lane. *Harper's Bible Dictionary*. New York, Harper & Row, 1961. Concise, conservative, and uninspiring.

Pike, E. Royston. *Encyclopedia of Religion and Religions*. New York, The Meridian Library, 1958. The busy person's handy reference book—brief and lively.

Roth, Cecil, ed. *Encyclopedia Judaica*. Jerusalem, Keter Publishing, 1971. Sixteen volumes. An excellent source for the Jewish view of New Testament events.

Steinmuller, John E., and Sullivan, Kathryn, eds. *Catholic Biblical Encyclopedia*. New York, Joseph F. Wagner, 1956.

Under General Reference I have not listed volumes that might be termed "religious interpretations" because this book does not concern itself with theology. I am making one exception by including four books on the Gospels in *The Pelican New Testament Commentaries*, published in 1963.

Caird, C. B. Saint Luke.

Fenton, J. C. Saint Matthew.

Marsh, John. Saint John.

Nineham, D. E. Saint Mark.
Lucid, interesting, and informative theological literature for the layperson.

NEW VIEWS ON JESUS

Allegro, John M. *The Sacred Mushroom and the Cross.* New York, Doubleday, 1970. Dull but didactic—for those who can wade through 205 pages of esoterica with a word index in Sumerian, Akkadian, Ugaritic, Semitic, Sanskrit, Hebrew, Arabic, Aramaic, Syriac, Persian, Greek, and some English. I am afraid to state Allegro's thesis: some aver it is a masterpiece of nonsense; others that it is a work of genius.

Ballou, Robert O. *The Other Jesus.* New York, Doubleday, 1972. An interesting assortment of narratives based on the apocryphal gospels not included in the Bible.

Bornkamm, Gunther. *Paul.* New York, Harper & Row, 1969. The general consensus of the scholarly world is that this is a "superb and masterful presentation of the mission and theology of Paul without equal." The layperson, however, will get mired in its theology and scholarship.

Brandon, S. G. F. *Jesus and the Zealots.* London, Scribner's, 1967. An amazing book written with force and clarity, delivering what it promises in the title.

————. *The Trial of Jesus of Nazareth.* New York, Stein and Day, 1968.

————. *The Fall of Jerusalem and the Christian Church.* London, S.P.C.K., 1951.

These two books tell you more about the essence of their subjects than a dozen other volumes combined. Brandon's scholarship is accented by vigorous prose.

Brown, Raymond E., ed. (and others). *Mary in the New Testament.* Philadelphia, Fortress Press, 1978. Though the authors are "orthodox" scholars not out to demythologize anything, these essays nevertheless give fascinating views of Mary as we see her mirrored in the new Testament.

Bruce, F. F. *New Testament History.* New York, Anchor Books, 1972. Answers most of the questions you never thought of asking as to what happened in that fateful first century A.D.

Bultmann, Rudolf. *Jesus Christ and Mythology.* New York, Scribner's, 1958. "The foremost proponent of the method of 'demythologizing' clarifies his revolutionary interpretation of New Testament materials," states a jacket blurb. True enough, but it is hard going.

Cardoux, C. J. *The Life of Jesus.* Great Britain, Penguin Books, 1948.

Carmichael, Joel. *The Death of Jesus.* New York, Macmillan, 1962. An excellent book on Jesus as a rebel. Clear and concise.

Cohn, Haim. *The Trial and Death of Jesus.* New York, Harper & Row, 1959. A brilliant theological and literary achievement giving the "Jewish" view of Jesus.

Craveri, Marcello. *The Life of Jesus.* New York, Grove Press, 1967. A scholar with charm, wit, and reverence for that which ought to be revered but with a jaundiced view of that which ought not to be revered.

Cullman, Oscar. *God and Caesar.* Philadelphia, Westminster Press, 1950.

Esiler, Robert. *The Messiah Jesus and John the Baptist.* London, Baptist Methuen, 1931. The scholarship is impeccable, the erudition immense, the material overwhelming, yet it has accumulated more criticism than lesser works on this subject—which only goes to prove that if one isn't going to agree with a thesis, it does not matter what evidence is presented.

Goguel, Maurice. *Jesus and the Origins of Christianity.* New York, Harper Torchbooks, 1960. Two volumes. Saint that man for an inspiring, original, and rewarding work.

Goldin, Hyman E. *The Case of the Nazarene Reopened.* New York, Exposition Press, 1948. Not recommended for fundamentalists whose most cherished suppositions might be threatened by this exciting trial in the modern manner.

Goodspeed, Edgar J. *How Came the Bible.* New York, Abingdon Press, 1940.

Grant, Michael. *Jesus, An Historian's Review of the Gospels.* New York, Scribner's, 1977. An excellent, balanced, objective historical review steering the reader competently through a maze of facts and dates.

————. *A Historical Introduction to the New Testament.* New York, Touchstone Books, 1972. A flawless production that tells you what it sets out to tell you without sermonizing.

Greenslade, S. L. *The Cambridge History of the Bible.* Great Britain, Cambridge University Press, 1963. Two volumes.

Guignebert, Charles. *Jesus*. New York, University Books, 1956.

—————. *The Jewish World in the Times of Jesus*. New York, University Books, 1959.

—————. *The Early History of Christianity*. New York, Twayne Publishers, ND.

Though aimed at scholars, these three volumes could also be of great interest to the layperson because of their challenging ideas.

Hoskyns, Edwyn and Davey, Noel. *The Riddle of the New Testament*. Two British theologians whose ideas are ahead of their courage to take them to the logical conclusion.

Kautsky, Karl. *Foundations of Christianity*. New York, S. A. Russell, 1953. A socioeconomic interpretation of the rise of Christianity that reads like an editorial in *Pravda*—a communist Jesus leading a band of revolutionaries against the capitalist establishment. Dreary reading.

Klausner, Joseph. *Jesus of Nazareth*. New York, Macmillan, 1959. A trailblazer. Has an excellent section of reviews of the main literature on Jesus.

—————. *The Messianic Idea in Israel*. London, Allen and Unwin, 1956. Should dispel any idea that Jesus was the first and only "messiah."

—————. *From Jesus to Paul*. New York, Beacon Paperback 1961. A penetrating analysis of the historical context of early Christianity, written with "a scholar's depth and prophet's passion."

Knox, John. *Chapters in the Life of Paul*. New York, Abingdon Press, ND. A well-presented study, though written from a strictly theological viewpoint.

Lehmann, Johannes. *Rabbi J.* New York, Stein and Day, 1971. An interesting study of Jesus as a rebel and an Essene, by a German born in India and educated in Berlin.

Loisy, Alfred. *The Origins of the New Testament.* London, Allen and Unwin, 1950. A scholarly, objective interpretation.

Mantel, Hugo. *Studies in the History of the Sanhedrin.* Cambridge, Harvard University Press, 1961. Only for dedicated students; but the last chapter, "Jesus, Paul and the Sanhedrin," is must reading for everyone.

Meeks, Wayne A. *The Prophet King: Moses, Traditions and the Johannine Christology.* Leiden, E. J. Brill, 1967. I confess I got lost in this most scholarly presentation. However, the last chapter, "Mosaic Traditions in the Fourth Gospel," is interesting.

McGregor, Geddes. *The Bible in the Making.* New York, Lippincott, 1959.

Pagels, Elaine. *The Gnostic Gospels.* New York, Random House, 1979. A new and challenging interpretation of the Gnostic Gospels revealing hostility to the early Church.

Phipps, William E. *Was Jesus Married?* New York, Harper & Row, 1970. The book does not discuss seriously the question of the title, for which there is no evidence in the text.

Reimarus, Herman Samuel. *The Goal of Jesus and His Disciples.* Leiden, E. J. Brill, 1970. Published in 1774, it is a daring, pioneering, original work in biblical criticism.

Renan, Joseph Ernest. *The Life of Jesus.* New York, Random House (Modern Library), 1927. A deft literary achievement that demythologizes Jesus with reverence while castigating the Jews with malice.

Ricciotti, Giuseppe. *Paul the Apostle.* Milwaukee, Bruce Publishing, 1953. Though written from a strictly Catholic viewpoint, it is an excellent basic text for an understanding of Paul's life and thought.

Robertson, A. T. *Epochs in the Life of Paul.* New York, Scribner & Sons, 1909. A Baptist view of Paul.

Sandmehl, Samuel. *The Genius of Paul.* New York, Farrar, Straus & Cudahy, 1958. A Jewish theologian examines the success of Paul.

—————. *A Jewish Understanding of the New Testament.* Cincinnati, Hebrew Union College Press, 1956. Recommended reading for Christians to get an outsider's view of their religion and for Jews to get an idea of what Christianity is all about.

Schonfield, Hugh J. *The Passover Plot.* London, Hutchinson, 1965. A book on Jesus as mastermind of his own crucifixion.

—————. *The Jesus Party.* New York, Macmillan, 1974. An interesting thesis that the disciples of Jesus constituted the avant-garde of a revolutionary movement that led to the war with Rome.

Schweitzer, Albert. *The Quest of the Historical Jesus.* New York, Macmillan, 1961. "The best introduction to the subject . . . a mystery story on the highest possible level," says the *Saturday Review*, and I concur.

Smith, Morton. *The Secret Gospel.* New York, Harper & Row, 1973.

—————. *Jesus the Magician.* New York, Harper & Row, 1978.

These two volumes tell the story of the discovery of

the "Secret Gospel" according to Saint Mark, with disturbing inferences about Jesus as a thaumaturgist and founder of a "sex cult," if this "gospel" is a true one and the interpretation valid. Great controversey swirls around these works.

Sunderland, Jabez T. *The Origin and Character of the Bible.* Boston, Beacon Press, 1947.

Wegener, G. S. *6,000 Years of the Bible.* New York, Harper & Row, 1963.

Wilson, William R. *The Execution of Jesus.* New York, Scribner's, 1970. An incisive, elegant work, where scholarship is hidden under excellent English.

Winter, Paul. *On the Trial of Jesus.* Berlin, Walter de Gruyter, 1961. Read it, read it, read it. The best book I know of that explains what took place at Golgotha in light of modern biblical scholarship.

Zeitlin, Solomon. *Who Crucified Jesus?* New York, Bloch Publishing, 1964. A Jewish scholar who concurs with the evangelists that a political Sanhedrin was to blame for the crucifixion of Jesus.

STUDIES ON THE DEAD SEA SCROLLS

Brownlee, William Hugh. *The Meaning of the Qumran Scrolls for the Bible.* New York, Oxford University Press, 1964. Rewarding if one is that interested in the Essenes.

Burrows, Millar. *The Dead Sea Scrolls.* New York, Viking Press, 1955.

—————. *More Light on the Dead Sea Scrolls.* New York, Viking Press, 1958. One view: sad saga of an excellent scholar buried by his own facts. A second: a spirited defense of the view that there is nothing new in the Scrolls.

Danielou, Jean. *The Dead Sea Scrolls and Primitive Christianity*. Baltimore, Helicon Press, 1958. Clear, lucid, incisive, and exciting—a must on one's reading list.

Dupont-Sommer, A. *The Dead Sea Scrolls: A Preliminary Survey*. Baltimore, Oxford, 1952.

—————. *The Jewish Sect at Qumran and the Essenes: New Studies on the Dead Sea Scrolls*. New York, Macmillan, 1955. Bold, brilliant, and original speculations on the meaning of the disputed scrolls.

Gaster, Theodor H. *The Dead Sea Scriptures in English Translation*. New York, Doubleday, 1956. Dr. Gaster guides you with a firm and learned hand through the labyrinth of the Qumran writings.

Ginsburg, Christian D. *The Essenes and the Kabbalah*. New York, Macmillan, 1956. An interesting museum piece on the Essenes, written in 1864, almost a century before the discovery of the Dead Sea Scrolls.

Harrison, R. K. *The Dead Sea Scrolls*. New York, Harper Torchbooks, 1961. A good introduction to the subject.

Lasor, William Sanford. *The Dead Sea Scrolls and the New Testament*. Grand Rapids, Mich., Eerdman, 1972. If you don't want to believe that Essenism influenced Christianity, read this book, which gives a good case for this argument.

Mansoor, Menahem. *The Dead Sea Scrolls*. Grand Rapids, Mich., Eerdman, 1964. An excellent basic textbook that competently guides the reader through the reefs of the Qumran scrolls.

Milik, J. R. *Ten Years of Discovery in the Wilderness of Judea*. Naperville, Ill., Allenson, 1959. Detailed and interesting, but more for scholars than lay-persons.

Roth, Cecil. *The Dead Sea Scrolls: A New Historical Approach*. New York, W. W. Norton, 1958. The theme of this book is that it wasn't the Essenes who wrote the Dead Sea Scrolls but the Zealots.

Schonfield, Hugh J. *Secrets of the Dead Sea Scrolls*. New York, Yoseloff, 1957. Dull but didactic.

Stendahl, Krister, ed. *The Scrolls and the New Testament*. New York, Harper & Brothers, 1957. Fourteen excellent essays on how the Scrolls have affected new thinking about Christianity. Though very scholarly, they are of considerable interest to the layperson, too.

Vermes, Geza. *Discovery in the Judean Desert*. New York, Desclee Company, 1956. Basic, but heavy going for the beginner.

——————. *The Dead Sea Scrolls in English*. Great Britain, Penguin Books, 1962.

Wilson, Edmund. *The Scrolls from the Dead Sea*. New York, Oxford University Press, 1955. The best brief, popular account that is likely to come our way for a generation.

——————. *Israel and the Dead Sea Scrolls*. New York. Farrar Straus, 1978. A potpourri of essays ranging from so-so to excellent.

Yadin, Yigael. *The Message of the Scrolls*. New York, Universal Library, 1962. An adventure story in scholarly detection. Also contains a fascinating chapter on the Copper Scrolls (related manuscripts etched on very thin sheets of copper instead of written on parchment).

PSYCHOANALYTIC INTERPRETATIONS OF RELIGION

Berguer, Georges. *Some Aspects of the Life of Jesus from the Psychological and Psychoanalytic Points of View.* London, Williams and Norgate, 1923. Interesting but not illuminating. No new psychoanalytic insights.

Cole, William Graham. *Sex in Christianity and Psychoanalysis.* New York, Oxford University Press, 1955. Fascinating interpretations of the unconscious motivations of sex in the lives and writings of Jesus and Paul, Saint Augustine and Thomas Aquinas, Luther and Calvin.

Freud, Sigmund. *Totem and Taboo.* New York, Knopf, 1939. A 161-page primer of the psychoanalytic interpretation of the origin of religion.

——. *The Future of an Illusion.* New York, Liveright Publishing, 1948. Freud's dour view of religion as an illusion but not as a delusion.

——. *Moses and Monotheism.* New York, W. W. Norton, 1950. The book that caused as much controversy as Freud's sexual theories: Was Moses an Egyptian prince who sold Judaism to the Israelites, in the same way that Paul, a Jewish tentmaker, sold Christianity to the pagans?

Fromm, Erich. *Psychoanalysis and Religion.* New Haven, Yale University Press, 1950.

Jones, Ernest. *Essays in Applied Psychoanalysis.* London, Hogarth Press, 1951. Though this volume con-

tains several interesting essays on religious
themes, the most fascinating is "The Madonna's
Conception Through the Ear," which explains
how an immaculate pregnancy could be achieved.
Muensterberger, Warner, ed. *Psychoanalysis and the Social
Sciences*. New York, International Universities
Press, 1955. Read Sidney Tartachow's essay "St.
Paul and Early Christianity: A Psychoanalytic and
Historic Study." Without destroying faith, it
gives new insights into the transformation of the
man.
Raglan, Lord. *The Hero*. New York, Vintage Books,
1956. Two volumes. A fascinating, objective,
non-psychoanalytic study of the hero in myth and
legend.
Rank, Otto. *The Myth of the Birth of the Hero*. New York,
Robert Brunner, 1952. Treats the same subject as
Lord Raglan's *The Hero*, but from a psychoan-
alytic view and is equally fascinating.
Reik, Theodor. *Myth and Guilt: The Crime and Punishment
of Mankind*. New York, George Braziller, 1957.
——————. *The Temptation*. New York, George Bra-
ziller, 1961.
——————. *The Creation of Woman*. New York, George
Braziller, 1960.
——————. *Dogma and Compulsion*. New York, Inter-
national Universities Press, 1951.
Fascinating studies on the psychology of guilt and the
need for atonement.
Rubenstein, Richard L. *My Brother Paul*. New York, Harper & Row, 1972. A psychoanalytic yet warm
portrait of Paul, clarifying many ramifications of
his life.
Schweitzer, Albert. *The Psychiatric Study of Jesus*. Boston,

The Beacon Press, 1948. It is customary to stand in awe of Schweitzer's biblical scholarship, but I found this volume somewhat dull and no trailblazer.

Spiegel, Shalom. *The Last Trial*. Philadelphia, Jewish Publication Society, 1967. I was flabbergasted when I read this; I could not believe that Jewish Orthodox literature could produce a book of such objectivity. It is a breathtaking journey of ideas about the *Akedah*—the binding of Isaac—from Talmudic sources, which unwittingly show a rabbinic understanding of Isaac as a forerunner of Jesus.

Wellisch, E. *Isaac and Oedipus*. London, Routledge & Kegan Paul, 1954. An absorbing study of the *Akedah* at Moriah, which permits one to perceive the future path of Jesus to Golgotha.

Zilborg, Gregory. *Psychoanalysis and Religion*. New York, Farrar, Straus and Cudahy, 1962. A sympathetic synthesis between Freudian psychology and Christian belief.

GENERAL WORKS ON EARLY JUDAISM AND CHRISTIANITY

Allegro, John M. *The Chosen People*. New York, Doubleday, 1972. Good history whenever his "mushroom theory" does not intrude.

Bright, John. *A History of Israel*. Philadelphia, Westminster Press, ND. An ordained Presbyterian minister views the history of Israel with detached scholarship and a few Christian-oriented speculations.

De Vaux, Roland D. *Ancient Israel, Its Life and Institutions.* New York, McGraw-Hill, 1961. A learned Dominican scholar who writes without bias.

Durant, Will. *Caesar and Christ.* New York, Simon and Schuster, 1944. (See especially Chapters 26–28.) As always, Will Durant writes with elegance and erudition.

Farmer, William Reuben. *Maccabees, Zealots and Josephus. An Inquiry into Jewish Nationalism in the Greco-Roman Period.* New York, Columbia University Press, 1956. A fresh look into an old problem.

Finkelstein, Louis. *The Pharisees.* Philadelphia, Jewish Publication Society, 1962. (See Herford, Travers R.)

Gibbon, Edward. *The Decline and Fall of the Roman Empire.* New York, Harcourt Brace and Company, 1960. (A one-volume abridgment.) Delightful reading, especially Chapters 15 and 16, which are masterpieces of polished prose and feature charming juxtapositions of irony with reverence.

Gontard, Friedrich. *The Chair of Peter: A History of the Papacy.* New York, Holt, Rinehart and Winston, 1964. One of the best histories of the Church I have ever read, allowing history to march side by side with legend.

Herford, Travers R. *The Pharisees.* New York, Macmillan, 1924. Written by a Christian and still one of the best books on the subject along with Louis Finkelstein's two-volume work, also entitled *The Pharisees.*

Hughes, Philip. *A Popular History of the Catholic Church.* New York, Macmillan Paperbacks, 1947. Though interestingly written, it leaves the reader with a curious feeling that while he has read a lot, he has learned little.

Josephus. *The Jewish War*. Great Britain, Penguin Books, 1959.

—————. *Antiquities of the Jews.*
These two volumes are available in an abundance of editions; two classics, still as indispensable today as they were 1,900 years ago.

John, Eric, ed. *The Popes: A Concise Bibliographical History*. New York, Hawthorn Books, 1964. Excellent biographical sketches of the popes with illuminating asides.

Keller, Werner. *The Bible as History*. New York, William Morrow, 1956. A lively re-creation of history in the light of archaelogical discoveries.

Marty, Martin. *A Short History of Christianity*. New York, Meridian Books, 1959. A Protestant view of Christianity, recommended for Jews and Catholics.

Moore, George Foot. *Judaism in the First Centuries of the Christian Era*. Cambridge, Harvard University Press, 1962. Two volumes. An amazing tour de force by a Christian scholar, accepted even by Jewish scholars as an authoritative work.

Osterly, W. O. E., and Robinson, Theodore H. *An Introduction to the Books of the Old Testament*. New York, Meridian Books, 1958.

Schurer, Emil. *A History of the Jewish People in the Times of Jesus*. New York, Schocken Books, 1961.

Smith, Morton. *Palestinian Parties and Politics that Shaped the Old Testament*. New York, Columbia University Press, 1971.

Sohm, Rudolf. *Outlines of Church History*. Boston, Beacon Press, 1958. A miniature classic, crisp and epigrammatic, recommended for Catholics, Protestants, and Jews.

Wellhausen, Julius. *Prologomena to the History of Ancient Israel*. New York, Meridian Books, 1957. Dull and pompous. This "great" biblical scholar of the 1880s has been "modified" into obscurity by subsequent findings.